# Handspinning

# Teach Yourself VISUALLY™

# Handspinning

Visual®

by Judith MacKenzie McCuin

BICENTENNIAL
1807
WILEY
2007
BICENTENNIAL

Wiley Publishing, Inc.

Library of Congress Control Number: 2007921818

ISBN: 978-0-470-09845-5

Printed in the United States of America

10   9   8   7   6   5   4   3   2   1

Book production by Wiley Publishing, Inc., Composition Services

Wiley Bicentennial Logo:  Richard J. Pacifico

# Praise for the Teach Yourself VISUALLY Series

I just had to let you and your company know how great I think your books are. I just purchased my third Visual book (my first two are dog-eared now!) and, once again, your product has surpassed my expectations. The expertise, thought, and effort that go into each book are obvious, and I sincerely appreciate your efforts. Keep up the wonderful work!

—Tracey Moore (Memphis, TN)

I have several books from the Visual series and have always found them to be valuable resources.

—Stephen P. Miller (Ballston Spa, NY)

Thank you for the wonderful books you produce. It wasn't until I was an adult that I discovered how I learn—visually. Although a few publishers out there claim to present the material visually, nothing compares to Visual books. I love the simple layout. Everything is easy to follow. And I understand the material! You really know the way I think and learn. Thanks so much!

—Stacey Han (Avondale, AZ)

Like a lot of other people, I understand things best when I see them visually. Your books really make learning easy and life more fun.

—John T. Frey (Cadillac, MI)

I am an avid fan of your Visual books. If I need to learn anything, I just buy one of your books and learn the topic in no time. Wonders! I have even trained my friends to give me Visual books as gifts.

—Illona Bergstrom (Aventura, FL)

I write to extend my thanks and appreciation for your books. They are clear, easy to follow, and straight to the point. Keep up the good work! I bought several of your books and they are just right! No regrets! I will always buy your books because they are the best.

—Seward Kollie (Dakar, Senegal)

# Credits

**Acquisitions Editor**
Pam Mourouzis

**Project Editor**
Christina Stambaugh

**Technical Editor**
Maggie Casey

**Publisher**
Cindy Kitchel

**Vice President and Executive Publisher**
Kathy Nebenhaus

**Interior Design**
Kathie Rickard
Elizabeth Brooks

**Cover Design**
José Almaguer

**Photography**
Matt Bowen

## Special Thanks...

To the following companies for providing fibers and equipment for this book:

- Andrew Forsythe (www.woolcombs.com)
- Ashland Bay Trading (www.ashlandbay.com)
- Carolina Homespun (www.carolinahomespun.com)
- Elemental Affects (www.elementalaffects.com)
- Lendrum Wheels (www.lendrum.ca)
- Patricia G. Scribner (www.patriciasyarns.com)
- Peace of Yarn (www.peaceofyarn.com)
- Schacht (schachtspindle.com)

# About the Author

Judith MacKenzie McCuin is a textile designer and teacher. She is a regular contributor to a number of fiber magazines and author of Victoria Home Video's *Spinning Exotic Fibers and Novelty Yarns*. She has taught and worked worldwide. Judith lives in Augusta, Montana, in the foothills of the Rockies, where she and her husband Nick have a fiber, yarn, and dye company.

# Acknowledgments

A book is never the work of one person and I have been fortunate to be part of a great team. Many thanks to my editors Pam Mourouzis, Christina Stambaugh, and Marylouise Wiack. I'm a better writer thanks to them. A special thanks to my technical editor Maggie Casey for her wonderful work.

Thanks to Jean Lampe for encouraging me to write this book, and to Jan Chamberlin for giving me the computer skills to do it.

Thanks also to Kate Larson, a brilliant spinner, who was the model for the photos, and to Matt Bowen, whose photographs are the heart of this book.

To Connie Kephart and Julie Bubp, many thanks for assembling the Web resources for me.

Thanks to Maxine Bronstein, Paula Rodgers, and Tricia Rasku for their beautiful knitting and weaving.

Thank you to Will Taylor, Andrew Forsythe, Jerry Jensen, Gordon Lendrum, and my husband Nick for the beautiful tools that make my work a pleasure.

Much thanks to my friends on the road: fellow teachers and students across the country on whose kitchen tables I have written and whose support has been invaluable.

And thanks to my husband Nick, always steadfast. Without his support it all wouldn't be possible.

# Table of Contents

chapter 1 **Why Spin?**

Why We Spun Then . . . . . . . . . . . . . . . . . . . . . . . . . . . . . . . . . . . . . . . . . . . . . . . .4

Why We Spin Now . . . . . . . . . . . . . . . . . . . . . . . . . . . . . . . . . . . . . . . . . . . . . . . . .5

chapter 2 Spinning Tools

Hand Spindles . . . . . . . . . . . . . . . . . . . . . . . . . . . . . . . . . . . . . . . . . . . . . . . . . . .8

Spinning Wheels . . . . . . . . . . . . . . . . . . . . . . . . . . . . . . . . . . . . . . . . . . . . . . . . .14

Spinning Wheel Accessories . . . . . . . . . . . . . . . . . . . . . . . . . . . . . . . . . . . . . . . .20

Maintain Your Wheel . . . . . . . . . . . . . . . . . . . . . . . . . . . . . . . . . . . . . . . . . . . . .23

Processing Tools . . . . . . . . . . . . . . . . . . . . . . . . . . . . . . . . . . . . . . . . . . . . . . . . .24

chapter 3 Spinning Fibers

Types of Fibers . . . . . . . . . . . . . . . . . . . . . . . . . . . . . . . . . . . . . . . . . . . . . . . .28

Protein Fibers . . . . . . . . . . . . . . . . . . . . . . . . . . . . . . . . . . . . . . . . . . . . . . . . .29

Cellulose Fibers . . . . . . . . . . . . . . . . . . . . . . . . . . . . . . . . . . . . . . . . . . . . . . .37

Specialty Fibers . . . . . . . . . . . . . . . . . . . . . . . . . . . . . . . . . . . . . . . . . . . . . . .38

Start a Stash . . . . . . . . . . . . . . . . . . . . . . . . . . . . . . . . . . . . . . . . . . . . . . . . . .39

Prepare the Fiber . . . . . . . . . . . . . . . . . . . . . . . . . . . . . . . . . . . . . . . . . . . . . .43

chapter 4 Start Spinning

A Spinner's Hands . . . . . . . . . . . . . . . . . . . . . . . . . . . . . . . . . . . . . . . . . . . . . .56

Spin on a Hand Spindle . . . . . . . . . . . . . . . . . . . . . . . . . . . . . . . . . . . . . . . . . .59

Spin on a Wheel . . . . . . . . . . . . . . . . . . . . . . . . . . . . . . . . . . . . . . . . . . . . . . .67

Troubleshooting . . . . . . . . . . . . . . . . . . . . . . . . . . . . . . . . . . . . . . . . . . . . . . .80

# chapter 5 Types of Spinning

Worsted Spinning . . . . . . . . . . . . . . . . . . . . . . . . . . . . . . . . . . . . . . . . . . . . . . .84

Woolen Spinning . . . . . . . . . . . . . . . . . . . . . . . . . . . . . . . . . . . . . . . . . . . . . . .86

Spin a Slub Yarn . . . . . . . . . . . . . . . . . . . . . . . . . . . . . . . . . . . . . . . . . . . . . . .90

Draft a Bouclé Yarn . . . . . . . . . . . . . . . . . . . . . . . . . . . . . . . . . . . . . . . . . . . . .91

Finish Your Yarn . . . . . . . . . . . . . . . . . . . . . . . . . . . . . . . . . . . . . . . . . . . . . . .92

# chapter 6 Ply Your Yarn

Why Ply? . . . . . . . . . . . . . . . . . . . . . . . . . . . . . . . . . . . . . . . . . . . . . . . . . . . . .96

Prepare to Ply . . . . . . . . . . . . . . . . . . . . . . . . . . . . . . . . . . . . . . . . . . . . . . . . .97

Make a Two-Ply . . . . . . . . . . . . . . . . . . . . . . . . . . . . . . . . . . . . . . . . . . . . . . . .99

Make a Three-Ply . . . . . . . . . . . . . . . . . . . . . . . . . . . . . . . . . . . . . . . . . . . . . .103

Troubleshooting . . . . . . . . . . . . . . . . . . . . . . . . . . . . . . . . . . . . . . . . . . . . . . .104

# chapter 7 Make a Cabled Yarn

What Is a Cabled Yarn? . . . . . . . . . . . . . . . . . . . . . . . . . . . . . . . . . . . . . . . . . . . . .108

Why Cable? . . . . . . . . . . . . . . . . . . . . . . . . . . . . . . . . . . . . . . . . . . . . . . . . . . . . . . .109

Cable with a Hand Spindle . . . . . . . . . . . . . . . . . . . . . . . . . . . . . . . . . . . . . . . . . . .110

Cable with a Spinning Wheel . . . . . . . . . . . . . . . . . . . . . . . . . . . . . . . . . . . . . . . . .112

Different Types of Cables . . . . . . . . . . . . . . . . . . . . . . . . . . . . . . . . . . . . . . . . . . . .114

Troubleshooting . . . . . . . . . . . . . . . . . . . . . . . . . . . . . . . . . . . . . . . . . . . . . . . . . . .115

# chapter 8 Spin Novelty Yarns

What Is a Novelty Yarn? . . . . . . . . . . . . . . . . . . . . . . . . . . . . . . . . . . . . . . . . . . . . .118

Color Variations . . . . . . . . . . . . . . . . . . . . . . . . . . . . . . . . . . . . . . . . . . . . . . . . . . .119

Textured Yarns . . . . . . . . . . . . . . . . . . . . . . . . . . . . . . . . . . . . . . . . . . . . . . . . . . . .124

Bouclés . . . . . . . . . . . . . . . . . . . . . . . . . . . . . . . . . . . . . . . . . . . . . . . . . . . . . . . . . .128

Garnetted Yarns . . . . . . . . . . . . . . . . . . . . . . . . . . . . . . . . . . . . . . . . . . . . . . . . . . .133

Encased Yarns . . . . . . . . . . . . . . . . . . . . . . . . . . . . . . . . . . . . . . . . . . . . . . . . . . . . .135

chapter **9** Spin Exotic Fibers

Alpaca and Llama . . . . . . . . . . . . . . . . . . . . . . . . . . . . . . . . . . . . . . . . . . . . . .138

Angora Rabbit . . . . . . . . . . . . . . . . . . . . . . . . . . . . . . . . . . . . . . . . . . . . . . . . . .140

Bast Fibers: Flax, Hemp, and Ramie . . . . . . . . . . . . . . . . . . . . . . . . . . . . . . . . .143

Cotton . . . . . . . . . . . . . . . . . . . . . . . . . . . . . . . . . . . . . . . . . . . . . . . . . . . . . . . . .146

Down Fibers: Camel, Dog Hair, and Cashmere . . . . . . . . . . . . . . . . . . . . . . . . .148

Goat Fibers: Mohair and Pygora (Type A) . . . . . . . . . . . . . . . . . . . . . . . . . . . . .149

Silk: Cultivated, Tussah, and Novelties . . . . . . . . . . . . . . . . . . . . . . . . . . . . . . . .150

Wild Fibers: Bison and Qiviut . . . . . . . . . . . . . . . . . . . . . . . . . . . . . . . . . . . . . . .152

chapter **10** Spin with Color

Introduction to Dyes . . . . . . . . . . . . . . . . . . . . . . . . . . . . . . . . . . . . . . . . . . . . . .156

Set Up a Dye Space . . . . . . . . . . . . . . . . . . . . . . . . . . . . . . . . . . . . . . . . . . . . . .157

Prepare the Fiber for Dyeing . . . . . . . . . . . . . . . . . . . . . . . . . . . . . . . . . . . . . . .158

Color in the Dye Pot . . . . . . . . . . . . . . . . . . . . . . . . . . . . . . . . . . . . . . . . . . . . . .159

Novelty Dye Techniques . . . . . . . . . . . . . . . . . . . . . . . . . . . . . . . . . . . . . . . . . .164

Spin for Color . . . . . . . . . . . . . . . . . . . . . . . . . . . . . . . . . . . . . . . . . . . . . . . . . . .166

Spin Carded Color . . . . . . . . . . . . . . . . . . . . . . . . . . . . . . . . . . . . . . . . . . . . . . .168

 **Use Your Handspun**

Knit with Handspun . . . . . . . . . . . . . . . . . . . . . . . . . . . . . . . . . . . . . . . . . . . .172
Weave with Handspun . . . . . . . . . . . . . . . . . . . . . . . . . . . . . . . . . . . . . . . . . . .178

**Appendix A: The Spinning Community** . . . . . . . . . . . . . . . . . . . . . . . . . .184

**Appendix B: Spinning Reference Materials** . . . . . . . . . . . . . . . . . . . . . . . . .190

**Glossary of Handspinning Terms** . . . . . .195

**Index** . . . . . . . . . . . . . . . . . . . . . . . . . . . .203

# chapter 1

# Why Spin?

We humans have spun from the time that we lived in caves to the days that we lived in skyscrapers. Whether it was a cord for a rope to cross a dangerous river or a yarn to make the perfect little black sweater, it all started with the same simple and timeless process of twisting fiber into thread. In this chapter, you will get a peek at the benefits of spinning—then and now.

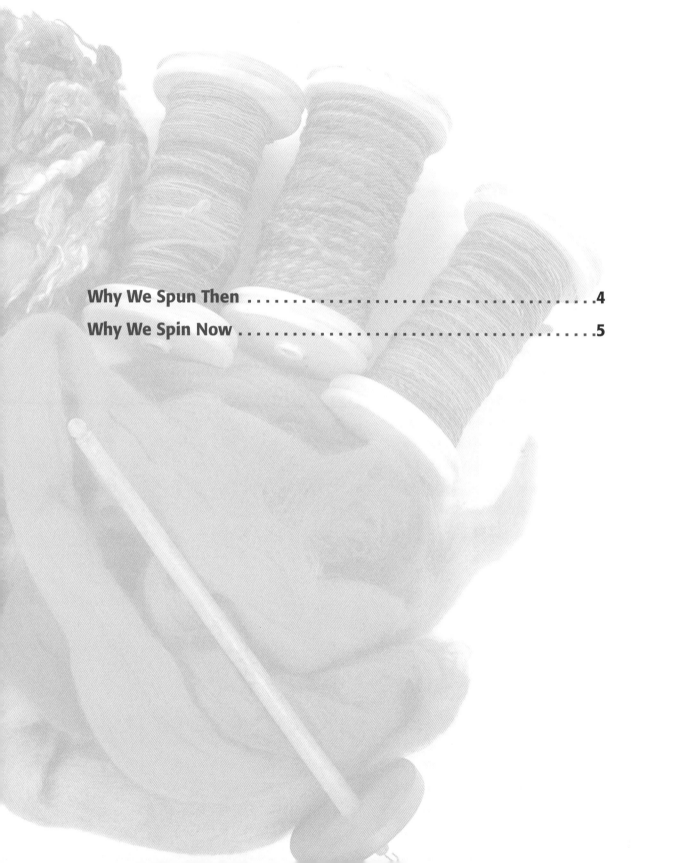

**Why We Spun Then** . . . . . . . . . . . . . . . . . . . . . . . . . . . . . . . . . . . . . .**4**

**Why We Spin Now** . . . . . . . . . . . . . . . . . . . . . . . . . . . . . . . . . . . . . . .**5**

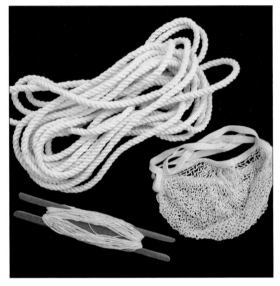

We have been spinning longer than written history. There are even samples of yarn spun from Great Woolly Mammoth hair. Originally we spun because we had to, and we made all kinds of thread, from strong to delicate.

We spun ropes for fishnets, cords to catch horses, cables to pull sleds, and sails to catch the wind. We used strong grasses, barks, and wild animal hair.

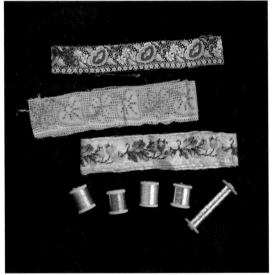

We spun thread that would make baskets to carry water and store grain. We spun thread to make blankets to keep us warm and to sew clothes that would cover us.

We spun for beauty's sake. We made ceremonial clothes and tapestries, yarns to embroider with, and yarns to make lace with. We made yarns from feathers, silk, gold, and silver.

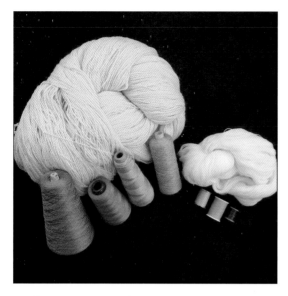

Modern spinners spin because they want to. Unlike pioneer spinners, who spun because they had no choice, industrial spinning factories have freed spinners to spin yarn that is unique and personal.

Learning to spin helps you to understand how thread works. No matter what you do—knit, weave, crochet, or make lace, quilt, or surface-design work—spinning helps you to choose the right type of yarn for the project that you are working on.

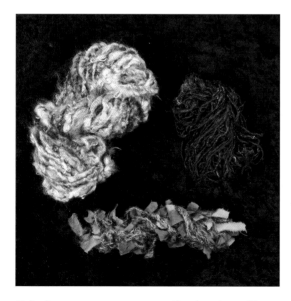

Spinning your own yarn opens the door to exciting possibilities that are not available with commercial yarns. You can use unusual fibers, such as yak and camel, and experiment with vibrant color effects.

Spinning is a great stress reliever after a busy day, akin to meditation. Spinning is also a great way to meet people, especially if you are traveling in a country where people still spin out of necessity.

# 2

# Spinning Tools

You use many wonderful tools in the spinning world. Some are as simple as kitchen forks, while others are as elaborate as handcrafted spinning wheels. This chapter is a guide to equipment; it will help you choose what you need to start spinning now. As you learn more about your spinning options, you can refer to this chapter to help you select the equipment that best suits the type of spinning that you want to do.

**Hand Spindles** . . . . . . . . . . . . . . . . . . . . . . . . . . . . . . . . . . . . . . . . .8

**Spinning Wheels** . . . . . . . . . . . . . . . . . . . . . . . . . . . . . . . . . . . . . . .14

**Spinning Wheel Accessories** . . . . . . . . . . . . . . . . . . . . . . . . . . . . .20

**Maintain Your Wheel** . . . . . . . . . . . . . . . . . . . . . . . . . . . . . . . . . .23

**Processing Tools** . . . . . . . . . . . . . . . . . . . . . . . . . . . . . . . . . . . . .24

# Hand Spindles

People around the world have used hand spindles for over 20,000 years, and they are still a good choice for both beginners and more experienced spinners. They are inexpensive, portable, and versatile.

While a hand spindle does spin more slowly than a spinning wheel, the advantage is that you can always have it with you. A few minutes of spinning during a busy day can produce a surprising amount of yarn.

## How They Work

Hand spindles make yarn by twisting fiber into thread. These tools are as simple as a stick and a stone. By twisting the *spindle* (the stick), you add the twist to the fiber. The *whorl* (the stone) is there to add weight to the spindle. This extra weight makes the spindle twist longer, thus producing more thread.

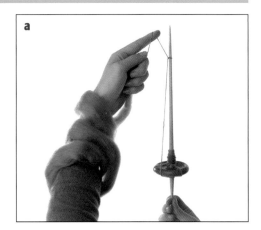

You can use a hand spindle in two ways: as a *drop spindle* or as a *supported spindle*. You hold a drop spindle (a) in the air. The weight of the spindle moves it toward the ground, and the yarn forms as the fiber is drawn toward the spindle.

You place a supported spindle (b) on the ground. The yarn forms as the fiber is pulled up and away from the spindle.

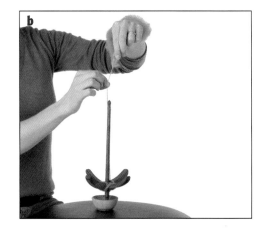

## Types of Spindles

There are three main types of hand spindles: low whorl, mid-whorl, and high whorl.

### LOW WHORL

You can use a low-whorl spindle (also called a bottom whorl) as a drop spindle, hanging in the air, or as a supported spindle, with the point of the spindle resting on a flat surface. Low-whorl spindles come in many sizes and spin both thick and thin yarn. They spin any type of fiber.

These spindles are found across the globe, and they're still in regular use in many countries, including Turkey and Peru, and on the Navajo Reservation. Spinners use low whorls to make yarn for Persian carpets, Navajo rugs, and fine silk shawls.

### MID-WHORL

Mid-whorl spindles are usually small and lightweight. Used for spinning fine thread, they are perfect for spinning cotton, cashmere, and other soft fibers. Spinners in Indonesia commonly use mid-whorl spindles to create silk and cotton thread for weaving.

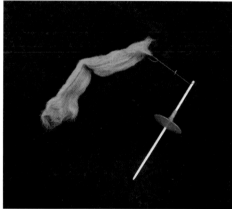

### HIGH WHORL

Probably the most common spindle used in America, the high-whorl spindle (also known as a top whorl) dates back to early Egyptian times. You can use it either suspended or supported, to spin medium to fine fiber, and to spin a wide range of diameters.

***CONTINUED ON NEXT PAGE***

## Buying Your First Hand Spindle

Hand spindles come in various sizes and styles. They can be simple designs or works of art. Many spinners collect spindles for their beauty and for specific types of spinning.

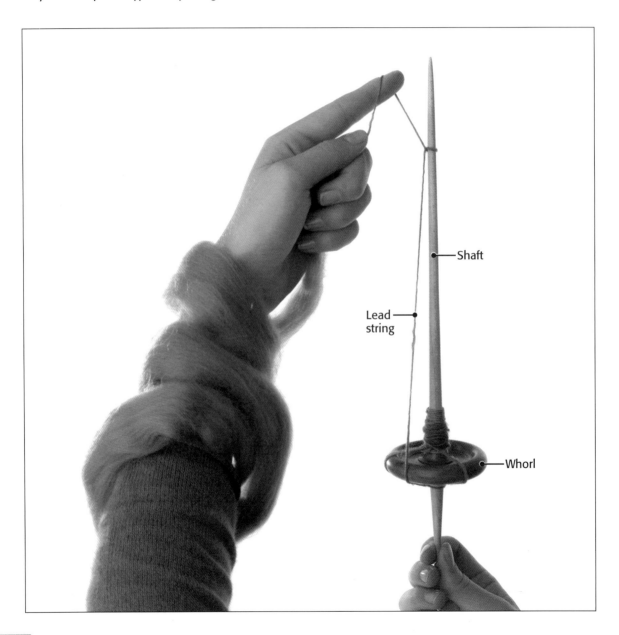

Shaft

Lead string

Whorl

## CHOOSE A STYLE

For your first spindle, keep your options open. Choose one that can be used in a variety of ways—either drop or supported, high whorl or low whorl. This will help you to decide which style you prefer.

## CHECK THE BALANCE

Rest the spindle in the palm of your hand, twist it, and watch it spin. It should spin easily and not wobble. It should also twist easily; the thinner the shaft of the spindle, the more twist there is in the yarn. Also make sure that the spindle feels good in your hands; for example, I prefer the feel of a smooth-textured spindle over a ribbed texture.

## CHECK THE WEIGHT

Spindles come in a wide range of weights, from as heavy as 6 ounces to as light as ¼ ounce. Heavy spindles are easier to keep spinning, but they produce a thicker, more loosely twisted yarn than a lighter spindle. The lighter the spindle, the finer the thread that it spins.

For your first spindle, choose one that is mid-range, between 1½ and 4 ounces. It is easy to keep spinning and produces a wide range of yarns.

*CONTINUED ON NEXT PAGE*

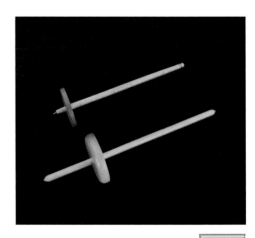

# Hand Spindles
## (continued)

### Making a Simple Spindle

Although spindles aren't especially pricey, you can make a simple one at home in only a few minutes and for less than $5.

To make a spindle, you need a CD, a size-11 knitting needle, two ⁵⁄₁₆ metal washers, two small, cloth-covered hair elastic bands, and craft glue or a glue gun. If you like, you can even paint the CD in a colorful pattern that changes when you spin it.

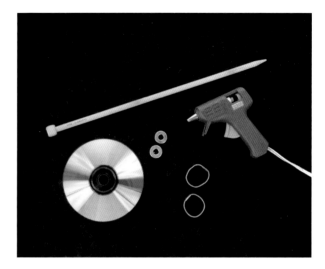

① Glue the washers over the center hole in the CD, one on the top and one on the bottom. Make sure that the holes line up.

### FACT

Historically, spindles were made from stone, clay, glass, and metals like pewter and silver. Spindles can still be made from a wide variety of materials. For example, you can make a lightweight spindle with a beautiful bead and a fine bamboo double-point knitting needle. You can also make your own whorls using fimo or clay.

2 Twist an elastic band tightly over the needle. Push it up about 3 inches.

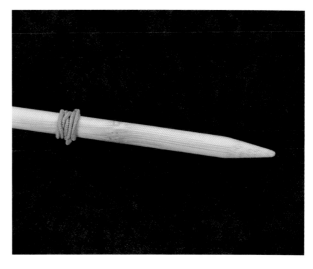

3 Slip the CD over the needle and push it up against the elastic band.

4 Twist the second elastic band tightly around the needle. Push it up to hold the CD snugly in place.

# Spinning Wheels

Spinning wheels started to appear in various forms around the 13th century—a short time ago in the history of textiles—and they have been steadily evolving and replacing spindles ever since.

Spinning wheels come in every size, shape, type of wood, and style imaginable. At one end of the spectrum, you can find antique parlor wheels with elaborate woodwork, inlaid with semiprecious stones and ivory, and at the other end, you can find high-tech metal wheels that run on electricity.

## Parts of the Spinning Wheel

### MOTHER-OF-ALL, MAIDENS, FLYER, HOOKS, ORIFICE, BOBBINS, AND STORAGE RACK

The top part of the spinning wheel is called the **mother-of-all** (1). The **maidens** (2) are the posts that hold the flyer. You can move them in order to put the **bobbin** (3) on and take it off. The **flyer** (4) is U-shaped, with **hooks** (5) along its sides. The yarn passes through the **orifice** (6) at the front of the flyer, over the hooks, and winds onto the bobbin. The yarn moves from hook to hook to allow it to fill the bobbin evenly. The bobbin moves more slowly than the flyer, making the yarn wind on the bobbin automatically. When all of the bobbins are full, you can store them on the **storage rack** (7).

### TREADLE, FOOTMAN, CRANKSHAFT, WHEEL, AND DRIVE BAND

Spinning wheels work like bicycles. When you put your foot on the **treadle** (8), the **footman** (9) turns the **crankshaft** (10), which then turns the **wheel** (11). The wheel turns the **drive band** (12), which then turns the flyer, the bobbin, or both together. (See "Types of Wheels" on the next page.) This turning puts the twist in the fiber and creates yarn.

### WHORLS, SCOTCH BRAKE, AND DRIVE BAND TENSIONER

You use these parts to adjust the speed. The **whorls** (13) change how fast the yarn forms and how much twist it has. They are located on the flyer and the bobbin. The **scotch brake** (14) puts pressure on the bobbin so that it moves either faster or slower. The **drive band tensioner** (15) controls how tight the drive band is. The tighter the tension on the drive band, the faster the wheel turns. The faster the wheel turns, the faster it pulls the yarn onto the bobbin. If the tension knob is loosened, the drive band will slacken and the wheel will turn slower. If the wheel turns slower, the yarn will be drawn onto the bobbin slower and will have more twist.

## Types of Wheels

No matter how elaborate or simple a wheel might be, it fits into one of three groups: bobbin driven, flyer driven, or double driven. Each type does one kind of spinning better than the others, but you can use all of them to spin a wide variety of yarns.

### BOBBIN-DRIVEN WHEELS

In the evolution of the spinning wheel, bobbin-driven wheels came first. When you put your foot on the treadle on this wheel, the single drive band makes the bobbin go around, pulling the flyer after it.

A bobbin-driven wheel is the fastest of the wheel types, but it doesn't offer you much control. However, this is by far the best type of wheel for spinning bulky yarns and textured novelty yarns, and for plying. Although you can use it to spin finer yarns, if you want to spin a lot of silk or cotton, this might not be the best wheel for you.

***Note:*** *For more on plying, see Chapter 6.*

One example is the Louet S10, which is shown here. The Ashford bulky spinner is bobbin driven as well. Most electric wheels are bobbin driven with the exception of the SpinTek and the new Ashford, which are both flyer driven.

***CONTINUED ON NEXT PAGE***

## DOUBLE-DRIVE WHEELS

In a double-drive wheel, both the bobbin and the flyer move. You have more control on a double-drive wheel than you do on a bobbin-driven wheel, but less speed.

Adjusting the tension on a double-drive wheel is easy because it has two drive bands. When you adjust the tension on the bobbin, you adjust the flyer tension as well, and they always stay in harmony.

Compared to a flyer-driven wheel, a double-drive wheel offers less control and more speed. This is a wonderful wheel for spinning large amounts of similar yarn and for spinning a medium to fine yarn.

Many modern wheels, like the Shacht, the Jensen (shown here), and the Ashford Traveller, can switch between double drive and single drive. Most antique wheels are double drive. In the evolution of wheels, this was the second wheel type to be developed.

## FLYER-DRIVEN WHEELS

This very modern type of wheel is the latest in wheel evolution. Like bobbin-driven wheels, flyer-driven wheels are single drive; one drive band makes the flyer go around. Another band, called a *scotch brake,* puts a separate tension on the bobbin. Of the three types of wheels, this one offers the most control over the diameter of the yarn that you spin and the amount of twist that you put in the yarn. Relatively speaking, it's also the slowest of the three types, and you need to be careful when you adjust the tension.

A flyer-driven wheel is perfect for fine spinning and for fibers such as cashmere, fine merino, and silk. The Ashford Traveller is shown here.

## Buying Your First Wheel

It can be overwhelming when you first start looking for a wheel, but buying a wheel is like adopting a pet: You'll know when you've found the perfect match. Try as many wheels as you can before you buy one; some stores and spinning guilds allow you to rent one. If you have friends who spin, try their wheels, too. You can use the list below to help find the right wheel for you.

### WHAT TO LOOK FOR

**Versatility:** Check that it can spin a wide variety of yarn sizes and textures.

**Simple adjustments:** Make sure that you can adjust the drive band tension. Check that it has interchangeable whorls that you can easily put on and take off.

**Wheel diameter:** Choose a medium-size wheel when starting out. A large wheel spins quickly and produces a high-twist yarn. Too small a wheel is difficult to keep going and might not create enough twist.

**Weight:** Treadle the wheel to feel its weight. It should move smoothly and not take a lot of pressure to turn. The drive band should also stay in place on all of the whorls.

**Left, right, or middle:** On many modern wheels, the mother-of-all is in the center of the wheel. On other wheels, it is offset to the left or right, to match the hand you spin with. There are several wheels that can switch the mother-of-all to either side. For your first wheel, a middle position is ideal.

**Style:** Part of the pleasure of spinning is the beauty of the wheel. Take time to look at a variety of wheels to find one that appeals to you. Also make sure that the wheel fits your body because you should be comfortable when you are sitting at it.

**Good working order:** Look for secondhand wheels, preferably ones that have been spun on recently. Spinning guilds and stores that teach textile arts are good places to look for used wheels.

As you learn more about spinning and become better at it, you might want another type of wheel; many spinners have more than one wheel. Stores often take trade-ins, and wheels generally have good resale value.

### WHAT TO AVOID

Handmade, one-of-a-kind, and antique wheels are risky buys for a new spinner because replacement parts may not be readily available and repairs may be expensive. It could also be difficult to find a teacher in your area who can help you with your specific wheel.

If you fall in love with an antique wheel, ask an experienced spinner to look it over before you buy it. It could have missing or broken parts that the seller, not being a spinner, is unaware of. Also, some antique wheels spin only a very fine thread and can't be adapted to spinning a wide range of yarns. Of course, you can have your wheel restored, but the repairs can be time-consuming and costly—perhaps not what you want in a first wheel.

*CONTINUED ON NEXT PAGE*

## OTHER WHEEL CONSIDERATIONS

### Double Treadle or Single?

Some wheels have double treadles so that you can control your spinning with both feet. You can treadle some wheels with either a single foot or with both feet. With other wheels, you must use both feet for them to work well.

For many people, the rhythm of a double treadle seems more natural, like walking, which may make it easier when you are first learning to treadle. However, double treadles limit how you can sit at your wheel; you must sit straight ahead, which sometimes limits how far back you can draw your hand when spinning woolen.

Single treadles allow you to change your sitting position. You can sit at an angle to the wheel that best suits the type of spinning that you are doing. Changing your sitting position can also help relieve muscle stress. There is some worry that using one foot might unbalance your leg muscles, but treadling is too gentle a motion to build leg muscles.

### Portable Wheels

Although spinning is a social activity, spinning wheels traditionally have been built to stay in one place. Many modern wheel designers build wheels that are compact and easy to transport. Unfortunately, some of the wheels' good spinning qualities have to be sacrificed to make them travel well. If you travel a lot, performance might not be as important as portability. However, the best traveling wheels make no compromise and work as well as traditional wheels.

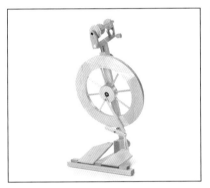

### Drive Bands

There are as many different drive band materials as there are spinning wheels, and the size and type of material that you use affects how your wheel spins. Some wheels have stretchy plastic drive bands. These bands are good for wheels that have a wide range of pulley sizes because they can fit them all. Other wheels have fine, hand-sewn drive bands.

You can change the way your wheel works by changing the drive band. Just slip the band off and tie it up on the back of the wheel when you are not using it. The heavier the drive band material, the thicker the yarn that you can spin. The finer the drive band, the finer the yarn that you can spin.

## Orifice Size

The size and texture of the yarn you are able to spin is directly related to the size of the wheel's orifice. If the orifice is too small for the type of yarn that you want to spin, the yarn will not pass through smoothly and it will become overspun. For fine spinning, too big an orifice can cause the yarn to jerk onto the wheel rather than drawing it on smoothly, even causing delicate yarns to break.

Most modern spinning wheels are made with a medium-size orifice. Some wheels have eliminated the orifice and use a hook attachment instead. Many wheel manufacturers make separate flyers for spinning specialty yarns. (See "Spinning Wheel Accessories" on the next page.)

## Hooks

Just like the size of the orifice, the size, shape, and type of hook makes a big difference to the range of yarns you can spin. Very fine hooks, closely spaced (as you would find on an antique wheel), work well for fine, evenly textured yarns but would be impossible for heavier or textured novelty yarns. Widely spaced hooks on one side of the flyer allow only thick yarns to spin beautifully but don't allow the bobbin to fill up evenly with finer yarns, which causes many tension problems.

Some wheels, such as the Lendrum (shown here) and the Magicraft, have a new type of hook that slides along the arm of the flyer, allowing the spinner to position it where it is needed to fill evenly.

Hooks can be L-shaped, cuphook shaped, or horseshoe shaped. L-shaped hooks are good for textured yarns, cuphook-shaped hooks are all-purpose, and horseshoe-shaped hooks work best for fine yarns.

# Spinning Wheel Accessories

## WOOLEE WINDERS

When you spin on a spinning wheel, you must move the yarn forward on the flyer from hook to hook to ensure that the bobbin fills up evenly. Traditionally, the spinner moves the yarn forward by hand, and you must stop every time you do so. A *WooLee Winder* doesn't have hooks, and it automatically winds the bobbin for you. The bobbins are wound evenly and firmly, so you get more yarn on each bobbin. Although this accessory saves time, it makes the wheel a bit less responsive.

It's easy to install (and remove) the WooLee Winder on your wheel. Unfortunately, WooLee Winders are not available for all wheel models. To see if there is a WooLee Winder that fits your wheel, visit the official WooLee Winder website at www.thewooleewinder.com.

## KATES

The purpose of a *kate* (sometimes referred to as a lazy kate) is to hold the bobbins when you are plying. Kates can range from works of art made of exotic woods, to very simple components made from a basket and old knitting needles. However they are made, kates all work very much the same. Some wheels have built-in racks to store extra bobbins. These usually do not work well as kates because the yarn is pulled out at an awkward angle.

**Note:** *For more on plying, see Chapter 6.*

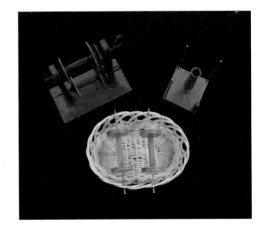

## SPINNING CHAIRS

Finding the perfect chair for spinning can be a challenge; it needs to fit your body correctly so that you can spin comfortably, and it needs to hold your body at the perfect height for spinning. Many wheel makers make special chairs to match their wheels. Most spinning chairs are lower than ordinary chairs, but if you find a comfortable chair, you can change its height to fit your wheel.

## SPINNING WHEEL TRAVEL BAGS

You can protect your wheel while you are traveling by carrying it in a spinning wheel bag. These bags are padded and have special compartments for extra bobbins and spinning tools, and usually have a carrying strap. There are bags designed for specific wheels such as the Matchless Schacht, the Ashford Joy, and the Lendrum folding wheel. You can also have a customized bag made or, if you are handy with a sewing machine, make one yourself.

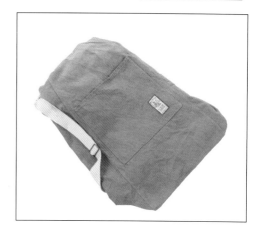

## LACE ATTACHMENTS AND PLYING HEADS

A number of wheels come with bobbins, whorls, and flyers that increase the range of yarns that you can spin efficiently on that particular wheel. *Lace attachments* are special bobbins and whorls that make it easier to spin both fine fibers and fine yarns. *Jumbo* or *plying heads* increase both the diameter of the yarn you can spin and the amount of yarn you can have in a skein. In some cases, such as the Ashford lace flyer and the Lendrum plying head, the entire mother-of-all is replaced.

## NIDDY NODDIES

*Niddy noddies* are used to make skeins. They are generally a standard size and make a 2-yard loop. Sample niddy noddies come in a wide range of sizes, but all are much smaller than standard niddy noddies. They are used to make samples during workshops and experimentation. Be sure to check the size of your own niddy noddy; some are metric.

***CONTINUED ON NEXT PAGE***

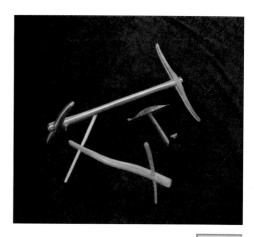

## SWIFTS

A *swift* holds a skein under tension so that you can wind it into a ball. An *umbrella swift* (shown here) is mounted on a table; it pushes up and spreads out the skein. An umbrella swift can also be used as a distaff for holding fiber while you spin or for stretching out silk caps. A *squirrel cage swift* is on a stand, and the skeins are stretched out vertically.

## ORIFICE HOOKS

*Orifice hooks* are used to thread the leader from the bobbin through the orifice on the flyer of the spinning wheel. Most wheels come with a fairly utilitarian hook, but spinners can choose from a wide range of handcrafted hooks. You can also make a beautiful hook with heavy silver wire and beads. You can find these hooks at most craft stores.

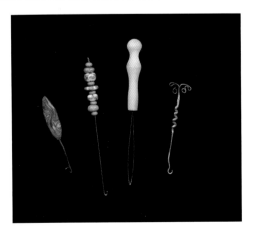

## DISTAFFS

*Distaffs* are used to hold fiber while you spin. Simple distaffs are made with a forked bit of lilac bush. Originally, distaffs were used so you could walk and spin at the same time. They were adapted to fit on wheels. Recently, many hand spindle users have made modern versions of *wrist distaffs*—a variation on a yarn bracelet—to hold your fiber as you spin.

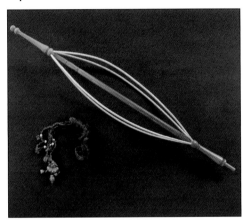

## DIZ

A *diz* takes fiber off a wool comb. It can be made of a wide variety of materials—everything from silver and gold to plastic milk bottles. Traditionally, horn and shells were used. A diz should have a concave surface, as it works as a funnel to help the wool pull off smoothly. You can also use a diz to pull off roving from the back of a drum carder.

With a little care, a spinning wheel will last you a lifetime. You can keep the wood clean by applying a little furniture polish now and then. While you are cleaning your wheel, don't forget the treadle, and turn your wheel over to check the underside. It works a lot better when it is free from dust and fiber.

Many wheels have leather parts on either the footman or the maidens, and sometimes on the bobbins. Keep the leather lubricated with a good boot polish or petroleum jelly.

Make sure that all of the parts remain snugly together and, if you travel with your wheel, take along the right size screwdriver to tighten the parts. If your wheel's tensioning device includes springs or elastics, add a few cloth-covered elastics to your spinning basket to act as replacement parts.

Oiling your wheel is very important. Oil every moving part, except for any plastic tubes. Oil is not just for lubrication; it also cleans out the fibers and waxes that accumulate during spinning. Look for oils with a low water content, like a sewing machine oil. A 30 wt. motor oil

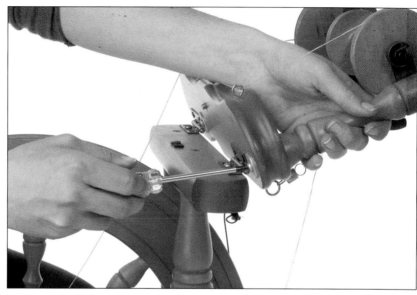

works well, especially one like Rotella that has a cleaner added to it. Check for oils used for mountain bikes.

Check that your drive band is in good repair. There are many different types of drive bands (see "Other Wheel Considerations" on page 18). For cotton or linen drive bands, look for frayed spots and obvious knots. You can sew cotton and linen drive bands together with a needle and thread, and use a little beeswax to smooth over the joint. You should replace your drive bands when they become shiny and smooth. Stretchy plastic drive bands can lose their shape, although you can cut and re-fuse most of them (use a lit candle or lighter to make this job easier). Make sure that the drive band is the proper length, with just enough tension so that it can turn efficiently. If you are adjusting the drive band on a double-drive wheel, make sure that the flyer stays relatively level in the maidens.

# Processing Tools

Processing tools help make fibers easier to spin by separating them and opening them up. The tool that you use depends on the type of fiber you are going to spin and the type of yarn you want to make. Or you may choose to not process at all; many types of fleece can be spun without being processed.

## Tools for Combing

### FLICKERS, FORKS, AND DOG BRUSHES

These simple tools comb fiber out straight and remove most of the vegetable matter that it may contain. They all do a very good job of processing long, shiny fiber. A *flicker* is a brush made especially for spinners, and you can purchase it where spinning supplies are sold. Forks (yes, I mean the kitchen utensils) and dog brushes can be found in most households.

### WOOL COMBS

*Wool combs* are used to process fleeces that are longer than 3 inches. These combs separate the long fibers from the short, weak fibers and organize them so that they're all straight. They can also remove any dirt or vegetable matter caught up in the fibers. You use wool combs to remove coarse outer hair from fibers and to blend colors effectively.

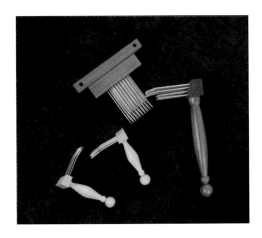

## Tools for Carding

### HAND CARDS

*Hand cards* are traditional tools for processing short to medium-length springy fibers. They come in a variety of styles, with curved back and flat back being the most common. They also come with different types of carding cloth on them: Coarse is used for more open fibers, medium is used for everything but superfine wool, and fine is used for fine wools and some exotic fibers, such as yak and camel. Some hand cards are made especially for processing cotton; these do a good job on cashmere and Angora rabbit as well. All hand cards can process fibers of mixed lengths. The hand cards shown here are cotton cards.

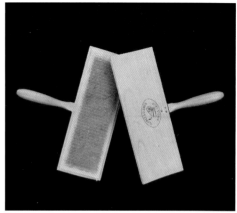

### DRUM CARDER

A *drum carder* does the same thing that hand cards do: It opens up the fiber and turns it into an evenly distributed *batt*. Although a drum carder does the job much faster than hand cards, and the batts are much larger, the end product is essentially the same. Drum carders vary greatly in the types of fibers that they can process without damaging them and in the amount that they can process per hour. Most drum carders are turned by hand, but there are electric models, too.

Drum carders vary in price, but they are all investments. Definitely try one before you buy one! (Spinning guilds often rent drum carders.) A drum carder may not work with the type of wool that you like to use, or you may not enjoy using it. However, it is wonderful for processing large amounts of fiber, and you can use it to make exotic blends and interesting color effects.

## Tools to Make Balls and Skeins

### BALL WINDER, NØSTEPINDE, AND NIDDY NODDY

All of these tools are used to wind yarn from bobbins. A *ball winder* and a *nøstepinde* (pronounced "NOS-te-PIN-dee") do the same job: They wind yarn into a ball where the yarn pulls out from the center. A ball winder is more mechanical and faster, but the end result is identical to a ball made by hand on a nøstepinde. As you learned earlier in this chapter, a *niddy noddy* winds yarn into a skein. Most niddy noddies make a 2-yard loop so that you know how many yards you have spun. All of these tools are available in a wide range of styles, sizes, and prices. Some are mass-manufactured, while others are made by artisans. Many nøstepindes and niddy noddies are made from exotic woods and are often very ornate.

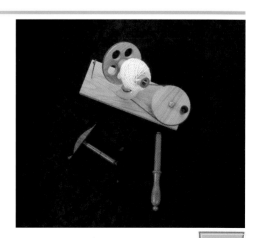

# chapter 3

# Spinning Fibers

One of the joys of learning to spin is discovering the amazing variety of fibers that are available for handspinners. Silk from China, cashmere from Tashkent, alpaca from Peru, and bison from North America—spinners today truly have the world at their fingertips! This chapter covers the many types of fibers that are available, as well as how to buy, store, wash, and prepare your fiber.

**Types of Fibers** . . . . . . . . . . . . . . . . . . . . . . . . . . . . . . . . . . . . . . . . . .28

**Protein Fibers** . . . . . . . . . . . . . . . . . . . . . . . . . . . . . . . . . . . . . . . . . .29

**Cellulose Fibers** . . . . . . . . . . . . . . . . . . . . . . . . . . . . . . . . . . . . . . . . .37

**Specialty Fibers** . . . . . . . . . . . . . . . . . . . . . . . . . . . . . . . . . . . . . . . . .38

**Start a Stash** . . . . . . . . . . . . . . . . . . . . . . . . . . . . . . . . . . . . . . . . . . .39

**Prepare the Fiber** . . . . . . . . . . . . . . . . . . . . . . . . . . . . . . . . . . . . . . . .43

Fibers for spinning are divided into two groups: protein and cellulose. They are divided this way, not because of how they are spun, but because they react differently to washing and dyeing. Recently, a third group—specialty fibers—has generated some very unusual fibers for handspinners.

# Protein Fibers

This group covers everything from sheep's wool to silk. Most spinners use this group of fibers because it is rich in variety and well suited for clothing yarn. In addition to wool and silk, protein fibers include exotic fibers such as alpaca, camel, and cashmere.

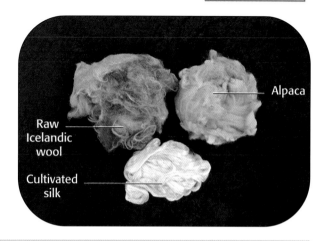

Alpaca

Raw Icelandic wool

Cultivated silk

## Wool

Shorn from sheep each year, wool is definitely a renewable resource. Our use of wool goes back thousands of years, and handspinners have used it to make everything from ships' sails to delicate lace stockings.

Wool is wonderfully lightweight and warm. Because it is *crimped*—like naturally curly hair—it is stretchy and holds its shape. This makes it an excellent choice for spinning yarn for clothing. The crimp also makes wool easier to spin, which makes it a good choice for both beginners and more experienced spinners.

Wool comes in a wide range of natural colors, from a brilliant white to the darkest black, and with many variations in between, such as warm-red browns, cool grays, and golds.

While many spinners love wool's natural colors, it is also one of the easiest fibers to dye. A wide range of simple wool dyes are available, both chemical and natural.

A downside to wool is that it needs special care when you wash it, as it can *felt* and shrink. You can treat it commercially with a chemical process that prevents shrinking. Fiber that has been treated this way is called *Superwash*, and this fiber is readily available for handspinning.

**Note:** *Felting happens when fibers slip closer together than their structure usually allows them to. Felting occurs, especially with many wools, when the fibers are subject to heat, lubrication (soap and water), and agitation (washing). Because of the rough, barbed surface, wool fibers can't move apart after they have moved closely together.*

There are many different types of wool, and each one brings its own character to the yarn that you make.

**CONTINUED ON NEXT PAGE**

## LONG WOOL

Long wool is silky, shiny, and very strong. The wool is between 3 and 12 inches long, and has a big, wavy crimp. Sheep in this group include Lincolns, Romneys, and Border Leicesters. Long wool makes wonderful yarn for socks, rugs, and tapestries, and is commonly used to make novelty yarns for shawls, scarves, and blankets.

## MEDIUM WOOL

Medium wool is soft, springy, and lightweight. Between 2 and 5 inches long, it has a lot of crimp, making it the perfect choice for most knitting yarns. Corriedale, Columbia, and Targhee sheep are all examples of medium-wool breeds. Often used for sweaters, blankets, and socks, medium wool is the easiest to spin and requires little preparation.

## FINE WOOL

Fine wool is the softest of all fleeces and is commonly used to make lightweight sweaters. It has a very tight crimp that is often so fine it's difficult to see. Although only about 2½ inches long, it is very elastic. It tends to contain more wool wax and grease, so it requires extra cleaning before spinning. Fine wool sheep include Rambouillet, Merino, and Cormo.

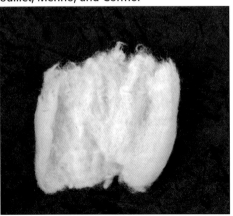

## PRIMITIVE WOOL

Primitive sheep are breeds that have remained unchanged. They produce a wide variety of fibers and usually have at least two distinct coats—a coarse outer-coat and a soft innercoat. Bred before we developed dyes, they come in a range of beautiful colors. Classic Fair Isle patterned knitting uses primitive wool. Shetland, Icelandic, and Navajo-Churro are all primitive wools.

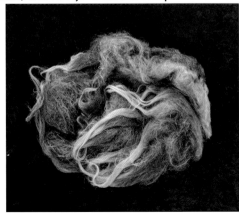

## Silk

Silk is the fiber that a silkworm spins when it makes its cocoon. Cocoons are collected both from wild worms and from worms that are specially bred and grown in captivity. Many countries produce silk—including Turkey, Japan, and Spain—but most silk comes from China, the country that originally developed silk fiber.

Silk that is used to weave fabric just as it comes off of the cocoon is called *reeled silk*. Handspinners use silk that comes from cocoons after the silk moths have hatched. These broken cocoons are then carded into spinning fiber.

Silk is strong, light, and lustrous. It is one of the longest natural fibers that we have. It dyes beautifully with either commercial or nature dyes, and it has a wonderful feel. There is simply nothing quite like it.

### CULTIVATED SILK

Cultivated silk comes from a special breed of silkworms, called *Bombyx mori*, which are raised in captivity. Unlike their robust cousins, the Tussah (see next page), these worms need a great deal of care. For example, they need quiet and cleanliness to survive, and they only eat white mulberry leaves.

Cultivated silk is one of the most luxurious fibers that we have. It has an incredible feel and is easily worn against the skin. The individual fibers of cultivated silk, called *filaments*, are very fine compared to other types of silk. Cultivated silk has a luminous, blue-white appearance, and it dyes very well, producing brilliant, glowing colors.

Because it is a much finer silk, cultivated silk is a little harder to spin, but it is well worth the effort. It is beautiful no matter how you use it, whether knitted, crocheted, or woven.

### SILK HANKIES, CAPS, AND BELLS

Much of the silk that we use is grown in small farms and villages, and processed by hand. *Hankies, caps,* and *bells* are all produced by boiling the cocoon in soap and water until it softens. The cocoon is then opened up, turned inside out, and stretched on a frame. Hankies and caps are layers of these cocoons, each of which is stretched on a differently shaped frame. A bell consists of layers of either hankies or caps, all bundled together. The yarn is very textured because the whole cocoon, from the rough outside fibers to the soft inside fibers, is all together.

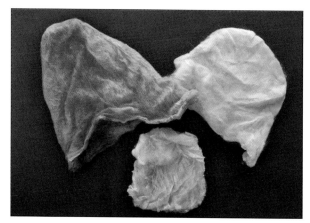

***CONTINUED ON NEXT PAGE***

## SILK NOIL

Although you might mistake silk noil for cotton when you first see it, when you feel it, you know that it is silk. *Silk noil* is the short, broken fibers that are left on the carder when the cocoons are processed to make spinning fiber. Sometimes called *raw silk*, it has a rough, tweedy appearance, and dyes very well. Silk noil makes a good knitting yarn and can also be used as a weft yarn in weaving. Because it lacks the exotic luster of silk but has all of the other properties, silk noil is a good choice for making more casual garments like T-shirts.

## TUSSAH

*Tussah silk* is gathered from a variety of wild moths. Tussah worms are big and robust, and they eat a wide variety of plant leaves. Their cocoons come in many colors, from pale cream to dark chocolate—but never pure, brilliant white.

The fiber from tussah silkworms tends to be uneven, ranging from very fine to coarse and wiry. Usually, the darker the color, the harsher the fiber. When tussah is dyed, it produces warm, honeyed colors.

Tussah is a good choice for your first adventure with silk because it is a little easier to spin than cultivated silk, and you can spin it into a thicker yarn. It is a good choice for making either knitting or weaving yarns. When you blend it into a sock yarn, it helps the sock wear better.

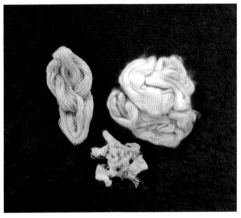

## Other Animal Sources

## ALPACA

Alpacas come from South America, where they have been used to produce exquisite fiber for thousands of years. Recently, they have become a very popular fiber animal in the United States, and a wide range of alpaca fiber, both raw and processed, is now available.

Alpaca fiber is often over 10 inches long, and is soft and lustrous. Its crimp structure can range from almost straight to very fine and highly crimped. It comes in a wide variety of natural colors, and fabric that is made with alpaca resists wrinkling.

There are two distinct types of alpaca: Huacaya and Suri. The Huacaya is more common and has a wool-like coat, while the Suri has a long, silky, and very lustrous coat.

## ANGORA RABBIT

Originally from Turkey, Angora rabbits are bred for their soft, luxurious fiber. One of the distinctive characteristics of angora is its fluffy appearance, and it produces a furry pile up to 3 inches long when it is used in knitting. It is frequently used in blends to make a medium-quality wool feel like cashmere. It is both lightweight and extremely warm, and comes in a wide variety of natural colors. However, keep in mind that it felts easily.

There are three main types of Angora rabbits: French, which has a furlike outer hair; English, which has a very fine fiber with little guard hair; and German, which is the longest and silkiest of the three.

English    French    German

## BISON

Once almost extinct, bison have recently made an amazing comeback, which has made it possible to collect and process their fiber. To survive the extreme temperature changes of the northern grasslands of the United States and Canada, bison, like yak and muskox (see pages 35–36), have five different coats. They shed off their fine winter undercoat in the spring, and this is collected, washed, and *dehaired* (the long, course outercoat hairs are removed). Bison fiber has just recently become available for spinning. Similar to cashmere in quality, bison fiber makes a wonderfully soft yarn for both knitting and weaving.

## CAMEL

The camel fiber that is used for spinning comes from Bactrian camels, which are found throughout most of Asia and are characterized by having two humps. The camels shed their hair in the spring, and it is collected and sorted.

Bactrian camels have three coats: The fine undercoat is very soft and extremely crimped. The second coat is similar to wool and is used for coat and suit fabric. The outercoat is coarse and wiry and is used to make tents and carpets.

*CONTINUED ON NEXT PAGE*

## DOG

Dog hair is one of the great untapped resources of the fiber world. Dogs that have a thick undercoat (like Samoyeds, Keeshonds, and Huskies) produce great volumes of fiber when they shed their winter coat. Sometimes the dog odor can be a bit strong, but a good wash in hot water and detergent removes it permanently. (For more on caring for your fiber, see "Washing Fiber" on page 41.)

While not as fine as cashmere or yak, dog hair has many of the same qualities of lightness and warmth, and it makes wonderful blends with silk and wool. Of all the undercoats, it is the easiest to spin and is a good place for a beginner to start.

## GOAT

### Cashmere

Cashmere comes from goats that have a downy, soft, undercoat that sheds in the spring. First used to produce exquisite shawls in the northern parts of India and Pakistan, cashmere has become one of the most sought-after luxury fibers. The fibers are very short, but because they are also very crimpy, it is fun to spin. Cashmere makes wonderful blends with either silk or wool, and it is the only commercial fiber for which the demand is greater than the supply.

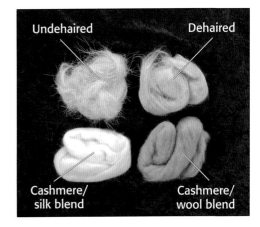

Undehaired  Dehaired

Cashmere/ silk blend  Cashmere/ wool blend

### Mohair

Mohair fiber comes from an Angora goat. Angora goats originally came from Turkey, where they were bred to make Oriental carpets. Next to silk, mohair is the most lustrous of the natural fibers, and, just like silk, it dyes brilliantly. Mohair is not only heavier than wool, but it is also stronger. It is used to make many novelty yarns, including brushed mohair and mohair bouclés.

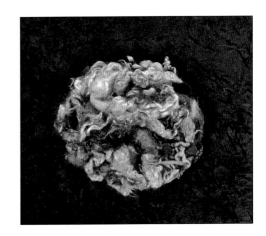

## Pygora

These miniature goats are a cross between pygmy goats and Angora goats. Pygora goats produce several different types of fiber, including one that is similar to cashmere (C), another that is akin to very fine mohair (A), and a third that is a mix of the two (B). These fibers come in many colors. Raw pygora fiber has a bristly coat that must be removed before you can use it for spinning.

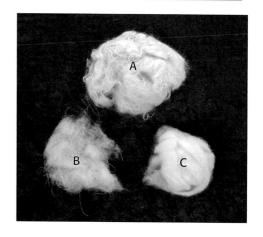

## LLAMA

Although they are from the same family as alpacas, llamas have a very different fiber. There are generally two coats: a soft, downy undercoat and a coarse outercoat that protects the animal from harsh weather. The double coats give the yarn that is made from llama a furlike surface.

Like alpacas, llamas come in a wide variety of natural colors. You can also purchase llama fiber that has been dehaired; the undercoat is as soft as yak down or bison.

First clip    Dehaired    Combed

## YAK

Yaks come from Nepal, Tibet, and Mongolia. As a result, they have great shaggy coats to protect them from the extreme temperatures of the Himalayas. Close to their skin, they have a fine undercoat that keeps them warm, and this undercoat is collected in the spring to make soft, warm yarn. It is available for handspinning in a dark brown, a gray, and a depigmented white. The depigmented fiber dyes very well.

***CONTINUED ON NEXT PAGE***

## QIVIUT

Qiviut, the downy, soft undercoat from a muskox, is the lightest and warmest of all of the natural fibers. At one time, muskox shared the great plain with wooly mammoths. They now live in the region around the Arctic Circle. Although the largest population is in Canada, there are also muskox in Alaska and Greenland. Like the bison and the yak, their fiber is adapted to the harsh climate.

Qiviut is often blended with other fibers, usually silk or fine merino wool. Although it comes in a gray-brown color, it can be easily dyed.

Because qiviut is warm and rather expensive, it is usually spun very finely for lace knitting or weaving. It is a challenging fiber for a beginner, but there is nothing as soft and as warm as qiviut.

## TIP

### Watch Out for Scurf in Undercoats

Animals that have undercoats, such as bison, Angora rabbits, yaks, and goats, can develop a skin flake in the fleece. A type of dandruff, this flake is called *scurf*. Check to make sure that the fiber that you buy is scurf free, because it does not wash out or come out in the spinning. If you have fiber that contains scurf, separate out the clumps of fiber that have scurf in them and throw them away before you start spinning.

Cellulose fibers are natural, as they come from the cell walls of plants. They represent the oldest group of natural fibers that mankind has used to make thread. With the advent of reconstituted cellulose, thanks to modern textile engineering, they also represent the newest group of fibers to be used. The four most common types of cellulose fibers are cotton, flax, hemp, and ramie.

## COTTON

Cotton comes from the fluffy fibers that grow around the seeds of the cotton plant. There are many types of cotton fiber—smooth, lustrous, harsh, wiry, soft, and rough—and they come in a wide range of colors, from pure white to dark green and blue. Cottons are found in both Asia and the Americas and have been cultivated since prehistoric times.

Because there are so many varieties of cotton, it can be spun into any type of yarn. When it is handspun, it makes a lovely knitting or weaving yarn. It can also be soft enough for baby wear and tough enough for industrial uses. Cotton is also very absorbent, making it comfortable to wear in hot weather.

Cotton is sometimes challenging to spin, but it is always rewarding. It comes in many different preparations (batts, roving, combed top, and so on).

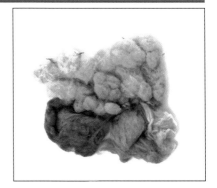

## FLAX

Flax, a tall, grasslike plant, has been spun longer than any other fiber. It comes from the skeletal part of a plant, similar to the stringy part of celery. Flax is easy to spin, and when spun, it is called *linen.* The strongest of the cellulose fibers, flax is used to make many things, including tents, tablecloths, bedsheets, and clothing.

Although it is difficult to dye flax yourself, you can buy dyed flax fiber for spinning. Its long, silky brown fibers are also often bleached white.

Line flax is the highest-quality flax, with fibers that are often 2 feet long, and a smooth, lustrous surface. Tow flax is the short, broken fibers that are combed out of the line flax. It is often blended with other fibers. There is a new flax fiber on the market called *twice retted*. It is short, like tow, but has the silky look and feel of line flax.

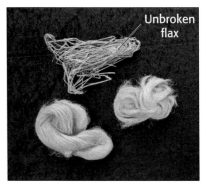

Unbroken flax

## HEMP AND RAMIE

Hemp and ramie fibers are similar to flax. Like flax, both fibers are found in the skeletal part of a plant. Also like flax, the use of hemp and ramie goes back well beyond written history. Hemp (photo a) is from the stalks of the cannabis plant (commonly known as marijuana). It grows much taller than flax—up to 14 feet—but the fiber is coarser. Ramie (photo b) comes from the stems of a bush; it is much shorter than hemp but gives a beautiful fine, lustrous fiber. Both fibers are very strong and are not damaged by water or sunlight; they are used to make strong, durable fabrics.

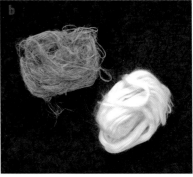

## MANUFACTURED FIBERS

Manufactured fibers largely consist of synthetic fibers. While most synthetics do not play a large role in the handspinning world, some, such as nylon, microfiber, and Mylar, are interesting additions to spinning fibers. There are also metalized fibers and even holographic fibers, which are blended with animal fibers such as wool and alpaca to add sparkle and color. Nylon is often used for strength.

There are also manufactured fibers that come from the protein and cellulose groups. For example, soy fiber and fiber made from milk are both protein fibers. There is also a new fiber made from seaweed that, like eucalyptus and bamboo, is a cellulose fiber. None of these fibers can be made outside a lab, though; they really are engineered.

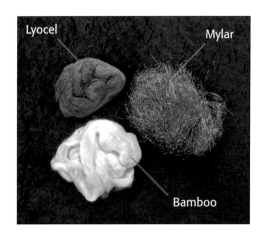

## BLENDS

Many beautiful blends are available. Cotton and silk, hemp and wool, and wool and angora are just a few of the blends that you can buy. If you decide to make your own blend, there is no end to the interesting combinations that you can create.

## RECYCLED FIBERS

Sari waste from India and Nepal is pure silk warp threads that are left over from weaving saris. It is available to handspinners and can be spun by itself to create a textured yarn or added to other fibers (for example, by blending it with black alpaca). A blend of cotton and recycled blue jeans is commercially available and makes a wonderful fiber to spin. Garnetted fiber uses bits of yarn or fabric that are blended with a fiber for a colorful, tweedy effect. There is also a fiber made from recycled pop bottles and wool.

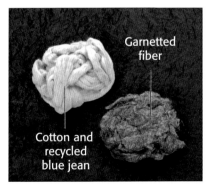

Every spinner has a stash—that wonderful collection of fibers that are just waiting for an inspiration. You can create your collection by purchasing a wide variety of fibers, and each one offers a different spinning experience. You can use the following information to help you purchase and care for the different fibers that you will use. You may also want to start a fiber log to keep track of what fibers you have, where you got them, and how you liked working with them.

## Buying Fiber

### RAW FIBER

Raw fiber is fiber that has not been processed for spinning; it is just as it came from the animal or the plant. You can purchase raw fiber that is washed, scoured (*scoured* means that all of the oils have been removed), or dyed. If you want to dye fiber, whether animal or plant, it needs to be scoured first. (For more on scouring, see "Additional Washing Tips" on page 42.)

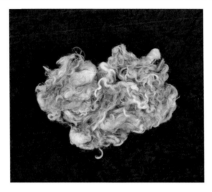

### CARDED FIBER

Carding is a process that opens the fibers up, untangles them, and distributes them more evenly. When fiber is carded, it's in big airy rolls called *batts* (left). The fibers are of mixed lengths and are crisscrossed over one another. You can make your own carded batts (see "Prepare the Fiber" later in this chapter) or buy them from a spinning store or wool-processing mill.

When fiber is carded at a mill, it comes in a continuous length, and is called *roving* (right). Carded fiber can be made from a variety of different fleeces and fibers, and it comes in natural or dyed colors. It is the easiest type of fiber preparation to spin and is a good choice for a beginner.

*CONTINUED ON NEXT PAGE*

## COMBED FIBER

Combing separates the fibers by length and strength, and any fiber that is weak, damaged, or short is removed. Combing also removes all of the chaff and vegetable matter. This process straightens all of the remaining fibers and leaves them lying side by side.

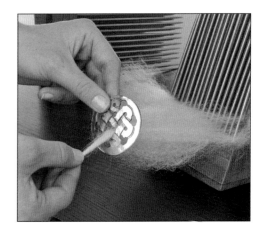

Combed fibers are called *top*. Top is more expensive than roving and is a bit more difficult to spin, but it produces strong, lustrous yarn.

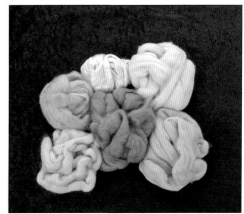

## FAQ

**How can I tell if the fiber is top or roving?**
Pull the fiber apart. Top pulls apart in a straight line; roving leaves a rough, triangular-shaped edge.

*Top*

*Roving*

## STORING FIBER

All fiber needs to be protected from moths, mice, and moisture damage. The most foolproof way to do this is to use plastic containers (preferably see-through ones) with snug-fitting lids. Avoid storing your fibers in baskets, brown cardboard boxes, or bags. These storage methods can house moths, which can eat an alarming amount of fiber. If you want to display your fiber attractively in a basket, then line it with heavy plastic bags first.

To find out if you have moths, look for a sandy, gray deposit in the fiber, and white, paperlike cocoons. You can use cedar, lavender, and other herbs as moth repellants, although they do not kill moths. Anything that kills a moth egg (for example, fresh mothballs and pest strips) is not good for you, so handle these chemicals carefully. If you have a bad moth infestation, then call a professional.

## WASHING FIBER

You should use a neutral-pH detergent to wash fibers. Fill a container with hot water, add the detergent, and stir. Add the fiber, gently pushing it under the water. Let it sit without agitation until the water cools, then drain the dirty water, and rinse the fiber in fresh, cool water.

If the fiber is really dirty, you may have to wash it more than once. You can get the excess water out by either using the spin cycle on a top-loading washing machine, or by pressing it out with a towel. If you are washing a small amount of fiber at a time, you can use a salad spinner to spin out the water.

*CONTINUED ON NEXT PAGE*

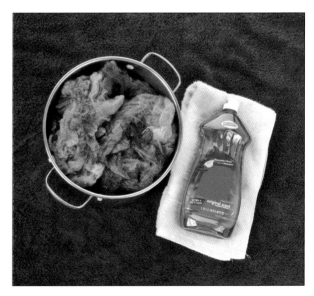

## Additional Washing Tips

- You can use a top-loading washing machine to wash some types of fibers, if you do it carefully. Lingerie bags are helpful for keeping the fiber intact.

- Crockpots are great for washing small amounts of fiber, especially mohair locks, which need a high heat to clean properly.

- Be sure that you rinse all of the soap out of protein fibers, as it can cause them to disintegrate. An extra rinse with a little vinegar is a good idea, especially for silk.

- If your water has a high iron content, wash your fibers by hand or in a crockpot so that you can use filtered or bottled water. The iron not only stains fibers, but it also weakens them.

- Wool can be hard to clean, particularly if it is fine. Wool has many natural oils and waxes; the two main oils are *lanolin* (which waterproofs the sheep) and *suint* (which is a natural soap that keeps the sheep clean). You need to remove these oils and waxes to process and dye the wool.

  Soak the wool for a day or two in water. This dissolves the suint, and removes most of the dirt. Rinse out the dirty water, and fill a container with hot water and detergent. Add the wool, let it sit until it cools, and then rinse in warm water to remove the waxes and the lanolin.

## FAQ

**How can I tell whether I got all of the oil and wax out of the wool?**

Occasionally, you may not remove all of the oils and waxes from wool. When this happens, the wool develops a gummy texture. Re-wash with very hot water and detergent. To test whether all of the oil is removed, take a bit of dry washed fleece and iron it on newspaper with a hot iron. If it leaves a greasy mark, then it needs re-washing.

Preparation determines the texture of the yarn and the ease of spinning. Flickers, hand cards, combs, and carding machines are types of equipment that help you to process fiber in a variety of ways.

## Types of Preparation

### TEASE THE FIBER

The simplest fiber preparation is to gently pull the fiber apart with your fingers. This is called *teasing*. When you are finished, the fiber should look like a big fluffy cloud. Teasing is often used to prepare fibers for further processing.

### USE A FLICKER

As you learned in Chapter 2, a flicker helps process long, silky fleeces of 3 inches or more. Flicking opens up the fiber without losing the fiber's natural structure. It also removes any weak or damaged fiber and most chaff and dirt. You can flick out fiber that is still "in the grease" (not washed), but it is usually better to wash the fiber gently first so the fibers are easier to separate. Place the flicked locks with the tips going the same way. (A *tip* is the end of the lock that is toward the outside of the fleece; the *cut end* is the end cut during shearing.) After flicking, the fiber is ready to spin. Locks are usually spun from the tip end.

1. Hold the lock of wool in your lap with your left hand. The tip end of the wool should face out.

2. Hold the flicker in your right hand and brush the tip out.

3. Turn the lock around and brush the cut end.

4. Stack in a bundle, keeping the locks facing in the same direction.

*CONTINUED ON NEXT PAGE*

**TIP**

Combing or flicking can be done when the fiber is still damp from washing. When fiber is damp, it swells and straightens, making it easier to comb. Combing or flicking when the fiber is a bit wet also prevents problems with static. If your fiber is dry, use a spray bottle filled with water and a few drops of mineral oil to dampen the fiber.

## USE MINI-COMBS

Mini-combs perform the same process as a flicker, with the additional benefit of separating out the long and short fibers, producing true top. They can comb fibers as short as 2 inches, and also separate out coarse guard hair from the shorter undercoat fibers in bison or qiviut. As with flicking, you can comb "in the grease," but it is better to wash the locks first. You can cut any sun-bleached or weak tips off with scissors.

**1** Use your left hand to hold one comb in your lap, with the tines facing up. Place the fiber that you want to comb over the tines, with the tips facing away from the handle.

**2** Turn the comb so that the tines face away from your body.

**3** Bring the right comb up and swing it down through the fiber. Let the weight of the comb do the work. The fiber transfers from the left comb to the right comb.

**4** When most of the fiber is transferred, pull the waste fiber out of the left comb and set it aside.

**5** Change combs. Place the comb holding the fiber on your lap, and use the empty comb to repeat the combing process. You may need to do three or four passes to clean out the fiber.

**6** You can spin the fiber right from the comb. Hold the comb in the hand in which you would normally hold the fiber. Draft up toward the wheel using a worsted technique (see pages 84–85 in Chapter 5).

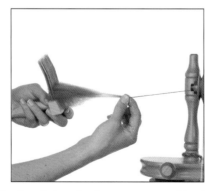

**7** Draft the fiber out until it stops pulling easily. Set aside the remaining short fibers. If they are reasonably free of chaff, they can be carded together with either hand cards or a drum carder to make a woolen yarn (see page 86 in Chapter 5).

**Note:** When you draft, you pull the fiber out of the fiber bundle into the diameter you need for the size yarn you are making.

## USE ENGLISH COMBS

English combs have been used to prepare fibers for spinning for centuries. Despite their name, similar combs are found worldwide. English combs consist of two identical combs with long handles and four or five rows (called *pitches*) of long, very sharp, metal teeth. They come with a frame, called a *box*, that is clamped firmly on a table. When a comb is inserted in the box it is held in place by a metal pin.

English combs are used for processing raw fiber that is longer than 3 inches. Combing works best on washed fiber. Carefully wash the fiber, and try to keep the fleece structure intact to make it easier to find the tips. It is also a good idea to keep the fleece in lingerie bags during washing. You can cut any sun-bleached or weak tips off with scissors.

Using English combs is a lot of work and they are expensive tools, but for a special project, English combs can produce perfect yarn.

① Use clamps to secure the box to a table.

② Place one comb in the box and secure it with the locking pin.

③ Load the comb that is secured in the box. Take locks of fiber and place them in the comb, with the tips away from the handle.

④ Take the free comb and pull it through the fibers, starting at the tip and working back toward the locked comb. Count the number of times that you comb through the fiber (you will see why in step 9).

*CONTINUED ON NEXT PAGE*

5 When the tangles are gone, unpin the locked comb. Turn it sideways and lock it in place again.

6 Take the free comb and comb through the fiber. This time, most of the fiber transfers from one comb to the other.

7 When most of the fiber is transferred, unpin the locked comb. Take off any remaining fiber and discard it (you can use it for carding; see page 48).

8 Change the combs, put the comb with the remaining fiber in the box, and repeat steps 4–7. Do this until the fiber is clean and open.

9 Here is where you find out why you have been counting. To make top, the fiber has to come off the comb, tip-end first. Take off the fiber on the odd-numbered pass so that it goes in the correct direction.

10 Use a diz (a concave disc with a hole in it) to pull the fiber off of the combs. Insert a bit of the fiber through the hole in the diz, with the concave side up.

**Note:** *The size of the diz that you use determines what size of yarn you can spin. When selecting a diz, keep in mind that you can spin smaller than the hole in the diz, but not larger.*

⑪ Using your thumb and finger, pinch the fiber as it comes through the diz, and pull the fiber and the diz down together.

⑫ Slide the diz back up against the combed fiber and pull more fiber down, using the diz.

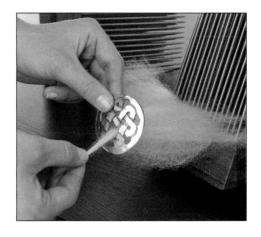

⑬ Keep pulling until the fiber stops moving smoothly. This means that all of the first-quality fiber is pulled off the comb. Take the remaining fiber off the comb and put it aside. Do not be alarmed at the amount of fiber that you discard—what is left is perfect. You can use the second-quality fibers for carding either with hand cards or a drum carder (see "Use Hand Cards" and "Use a Drum Carder" later in this chapter).

**CONTINUED ON NEXT PAGE**

## TIP

A new innovative set of combs enables you to make multicolored top by blending commercially died merino. One is a traditional English comb and the second, which is always stationary, is a *hackle* (a comb without a handle). To use these combs:

1. Start with three merino fibers of intense color.

2. Place them on bands in the hackle.

3. Comb through them to remove any tangles.

4. Diz off the size that you want to spin.

## USE HAND CARDS

Hand cards are used to process fiber that is less than 3 inches long. Fiber that you process on hand cards is soft, open, and easy to spin.

**1** Sit in a comfortable chair. Hold one of the cards in your left hand, and place it on your left knee with the teeth up.

**2** Take a handful of teased fiber (see page 43) and catch it in the teeth of the card. Just put a little bit of fiber on at a time; too much fiber makes it harder to card.

**3** Hold the other card in your right hand (if you are left-handed, just reverse your hand positions). Stroke the fiber gently with the carder, as if you were stroking a cat. Make sure that the bottom (where the handle is) of the right card starts the stroke at the bottom of the left card. As you stroke, most of the fiber should pass from the left card to the right carder.

**4** Transfer the fiber from the left card to the right card. Take the bottom of the right card, and place it at the top of the left card. Sweep the right carder down the face of the left one.

**5** Transfer the fiber back to the left carder. Place the bottom of the left carder on the top of the right carder, and swoop down. The fiber should now be back on the left carder.

**6** Continue from left to right until the fiber is quite open and evenly distributed.

**7** Remove the fiber from the card by transferring it from left to right quickly. Lay a card in your lap upside down. Place the fiber on the card.

**8** Take a knitting needle or piece of dowel, place it on the fiber at the top of the card, and roll it away from you. The fiber should wrap around the dowel.

**9** Push the fiber off the dowel. This is called a *rolag* and is ready to spin. To add an extra twist, you can tighten the rolag by pressing it with your thumb while you twist the stick. This is called a *puni*, and is often used for spinning cotton.

***CONTINUED ON NEXT PAGE***

## Tips for Hand Carding

**Hand card different colors of fiber together.** You can add color in bands on the carder. Keep track of the width of the bands if you want to make the rolags match. Watch the colors mix to create a new color as you pass from carder to carder.

**Use the hand cards to create a garnetted blend (see page 38).** Take a handful of llama and catch it in the teeth of the cards. Cut the silk waste to an inch, sprinkle it on top, and card the fibers together. Take them off as rolags.

## FAQ

**I noticed that not all hand cards have the same type of carding cloth on them. Which cloth is best?**

Hand cards come in a wide variety of carding cloth types. The cloth varies by the size of the teeth, how closely the teeth are set together, and the angle of the bend in the teeth. Usually, the finer the teeth and more closely set together they are, the finer the fiber is that can be carded on them. The more pronounced the bend in the teeth, the more gentle the carding action. Often, spinners have more than one set of cards, using coarse cards for strong wools and fine cards for cotton and cashmere.

## USE A DRUM CARDER

Drum carders do essentially the same job as hand cards. The advantage of a drum carder is how much quicker it can process fiber. The disadvantage is that drum carders are relatively expensive. If you plan to process large amounts of fiber, a drum carder is a good investment. They also allow you to prepare more fiber at one time and to make larger batts. They can be turned by hand or with an electric motor. Electric drum carders give you the advantage of speed, and free your hands so that you can easily feed the fiber into the carder.

1. Lightly tease the washed fiber apart, and place it on the bed of the carder.

2. As you turn the drums, the fiber should be drawn in. The teeth on both drums comb the fiber apart. Place the fiber so that the back drum fills up evenly.

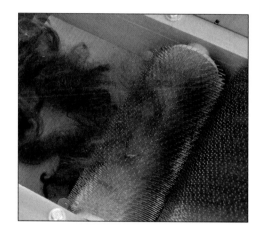

**Note:** *Some carders come with an attachment that allows you to press the fiber into the teeth in order to make a dense batt. If you do not have this attachment, use a floor brush and press it along the drum as the drum turns.*

***CONTINUED ON NEXT PAGE***

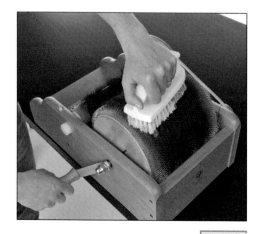

**3** When the back drum is full, the fiber should show above the carding cloth teeth. Use the *doffer* (a sturdy metal rod with a handle; it usually comes with the carder but not always) to take off the batt. Run the doffer along the groove that is left at the end seam of the carding cloth.

**4** Lift up the doffer and the fiber will come loose.

**5** Take a *slicker* or a dowel and roll off the batt. (A slicker is a wooden dowel with a plastic sheet attached to it. By catching the loose end of the fiber around the dowel and rolling it tight, the slicker lifts the fiber out of the carding teeth and keeps the batt in perfect order.)

**6** Fold the batt in half and roll it up. It is now ready to spin.

7 Clean off the front roller (called the *licker in*) with a dog brush.

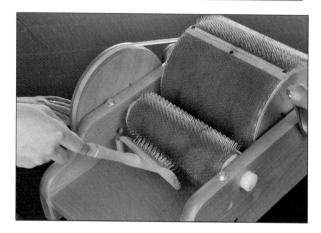

## TIP

### Adjusting the Drums

You can move the drums on carders a bit closer or farther apart for different fibers. The closer the teeth, the more vigorous the carding will be; the farther apart, the more delicate it will be. The fiber will be carded faster if the teeth are close together, but it will have to be a sturdy fiber—mohair, Romney, or Lincoln, for instance. For delicate fibers like cashmere, fine wools, and Angora rabbit, try setting the drums farther apart. For most carders, a credit-card thickness is the ideal distance between the teeth.

# chapter 4

# Start Spinning

Spinning can be a great adventure, and learning to spin gives you the skill to produce wonderful and unique yarns. It can be a personal expression of your creativity, whether it is through knitting, crocheting, or weaving. When you spin, you gain a much better understanding of yarn and fabrics—how they work and what you can do with them.

In this chapter, you learn how to make a simple yarn using a hand spindle. Once you learn the basic hand motions, you then learn how to spin yarn on a spinning wheel. You can use the troubleshooting guide to help you adjust both yourself and your spinning equipment to create the yarn that you want. Now, are you ready to spin?

A Spinner's Hands . . . . . . . . . . . . . . . . . . . . . . . . . . . . . . . . .56

Spin on a Hand Spindle . . . . . . . . . . . . . . . . . . . . . . . . . . . . .59

Spin on a Wheel . . . . . . . . . . . . . . . . . . . . . . . . . . . . . . . . . .67

Troubleshooting . . . . . . . . . . . . . . . . . . . . . . . . . . . . . . . . . .80

# A Spinner's Hands

The human hand is an amazing tool. Our hands have strength, sensitivity, and memory, and they tell us more about the world than all of the other sensory organs in our body. They also enable us to build our world.

Making and using tools are skills that define us as human. One of the earliest tools that humans created was a hand spindle. In fact, hand spindles go back so far in time that we have spindles with mammoth yarn spun on them.

## Right or Left?

You have very different muscles in your left and right hands, and each hand is designed for specific types of tasks. If you are right-handed, you have most of your fine motor-skill muscles in your right hand. If you are left-handed, you have most of these muscles in your left hand.

No matter what method of spinning you are using, the hand that controls the twist is the hand that needs fine motor skills. The hand that holds the fiber needs to be sensitive to movement and pressure. For example, if you are right-handed, you can spin with your right hand and hold the fiber in your left hand, and if you are left-handed, you can hold the fiber in your right hand and do the spinning with your left hand. This matches the pattern of skills that your brain has set up.

In this book, we use the terms *fiber hand* and *spinning hand* to describe the hand positions.

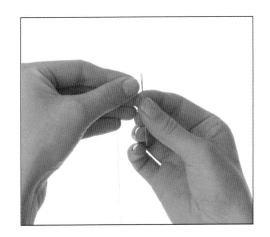

## Warm-ups and Stretches

### WARM-UPS

The warm-ups and stretches described below transfer blood and warmth to the muscles and tendons, which makes them more flexible.

1. Spread your fingers wide apart.

2. Starting with the little finger, roll them down to your palm. Do not forget to roll in the thumb.

3. Repeat ten times.

1. Put your fingers together.

2. Slowly roll your fingers toward the palm. Make a fist.

3. Slowly continue rolling toward the inside of your wrist.

4. Repeat ten times.

### STRETCHES

Use this stretch to keep the kinks out of your shoulder and neck, as well as to relieve tension in your arms and hands. You need a skein of yarn to perform this stretch.

1. Take a skein of yarn and hold it over your shoulder with one hand.

2. Reach behind your back with the other hand and catch the end of the skein.

3. Give a good, steady pull with both hands.

4. Reverse your hands and repeat.

continued notice

*CONTINUED ON NEXT PAGE*

Use this stretch to help relieve tension or pressure in your wrist.

**1** Stand next to a wall with your body parallel to the wall. Raise your arm from your side to shoulder height and extend your arm to reach the wall.

**2** Place the flat of your palm against the wall, fingers pointing toward the floor.

**3** From your fingertips to your palm, gently press down until you have as much contact with the wall as you can.

**4** Slowly turn your head away from the wall until you feel pressure. Count to 60. Release.

**5** Reverse sides and repeat.

## FAQ

**I do some things right-handed and others left-handed. Is there a way to tell if I am a right- or left-handed spinner?**

You may not be sure which of your hands is truly dominant. Our society favors right-handed people, and as a result, many left-handers adapt. Use this simple way to check for left- or right-handedness.

Imagine threading a sewing needle. If you hold the needle in your left hand and the thread in your right, you are likely right-handed. If you hold the needle in your right hand and the thread in your left (as in the photo on page 56), you are most likely left-handed. Interestingly, if you hold the needle in your left hand and the thread in your right hand, and place the needle onto the thread, you are very left-handed.

If you are able to use both hands equally, then pick one for holding the fiber and one for spinning. Your hands are able to develop the correct muscles and memory for the work that they will do.

# Spin on a Hand Spindle

To get started, you need a medium-weight hand spindle and ½ pound of medium (curded) roving—Corriedale, if possible. You also need 18 inches of commercial two-ply yarn. You will use this yarn, called a *leader,* to connect the spindle and the fiber. You must attach the leader snugly to the spindle with a slipknot.

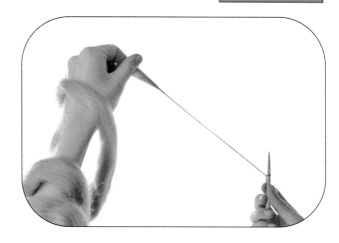

## Set Up the Spindle

### ATTACH THE LEADER TO THE SPINDLE

Use two simple knots to attach the leader to the spindle: first, a slipknot and then, a half-hitch knot. The steps below help you to make the knots and to prepare your spindle for spinning.

### TO MAKE A SLIPKNOT

1 Take the two-ply yarn (a single strand will come apart as the spindle turns) and wrap it around your finger so that the long end crosses the short end.

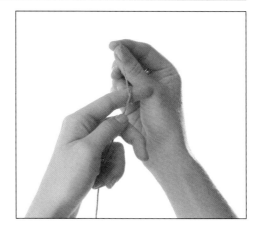

2 Slip the yarn off your finger and hold it between your thumb and finger.

*CONTINUED ON NEXT PAGE*

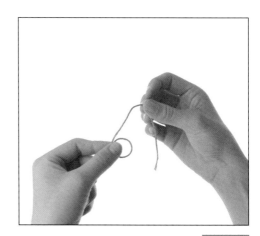

**3** Pull the long end through the circle as a big loop.

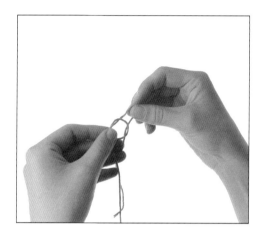

**4** Slip this big loop over the shaft of the spindle and slide it down to the whorl. Pull the loose end to make it fit snugly.

**5** Wrap the long end of the leader around the bottom of the spindle several times.

**6** Bring it back up the shaft and make a half-hitch knot.

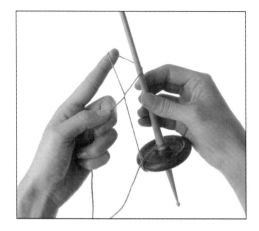

## TO MAKE A HALF-HITCH KNOT

**1** Make a loop with the loose end on top of the leader. Hold it between your fingers.

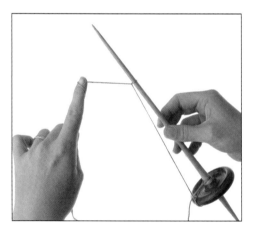

**2** Turn it over so that the leader is now on top. Slip the loop over the top of the spindle shaft and pull it tight. The spindle should be able to hang by the leader.

Some spindles have a hook at the end. If your spindle has one of these, you do not need to make a half-hitch knot. Instead, simply run the leader through the hook.

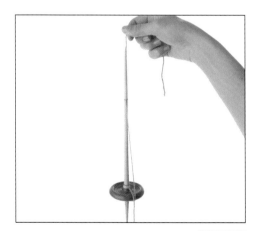

***CONTINUED ON NEXT PAGE***

## Spin

### START THE SPINDLE

To start spinning with a hand spindle, you must be standing up. This is because standing gives you a bit more time to draft out the fibers. When you become more experienced, you can sit and spin with a spindle.

1 Take the end of the leader in your fiber hand, and let the spindle hang free.

2 Reach down with your spinning hand and twist the spindle with your fingers and thumb so that it turns to the right. Practice this a few times before you add the fiber.

You may find that the spindle spins first to the right and then dramatically turns back to the left. This happens when the leader has so much twist in it that it cannot twist to the right any more. It also happens when you are spinning. Just let it unwind a bit by itself, and then give it another twist to the right.

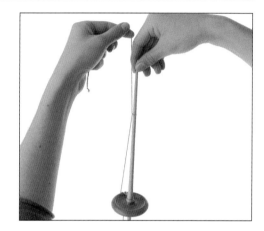

### READY TO SPIN

1 Gather up your fiber and determine which direction pulls out most easily.

2 Tuck the fiber under your arm or wrap it around your wrist.

3 Bring it through the palm of your hand. The loose end should come over your first finger, and your thumb holds the fiber in place.

### CONNECT THE FIBER TO THE LEADER

4 Lay about 10 inches of the leader across the fiber. It should pass over the roving and be held gently in place with your thumb. The spindle should be hanging free.

5 Reach down and give the spindle a firm twist to the right.

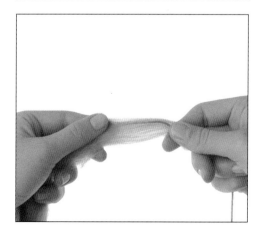

## TRANSFER THE TWIST TO THE FIBER

⑥ You should feel—and see—the twist come up the leader. When it reaches the fiber, the fiber should start to twist.

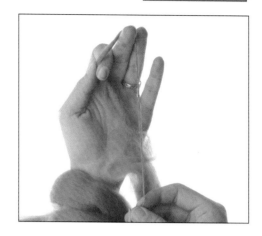

## STRETCH OUT THE FIBER

⑦ Tighten your thumb and finger on your spinning hand. Pull both the leader and the fiber forward (toward the spindle) together. Do not let the twist enter the fiber until you have pulled out about 3 inches.

## ENTER IN THE TWIST

⑧ Relax your spinning fingers slightly. Move them smoothly up the stretched-out fiber and leader, back toward your fiber hand. Watch the twist follow your fingers up the thread.

⑨ Tighten the fingers on your fiber hand so that the twist cannot get into the fibers that are not stretched out.

*CONTINUED ON NEXT PAGE*

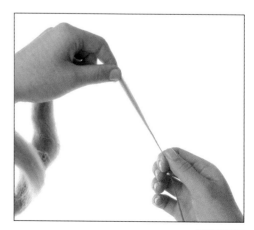

## DRAFT OUT MORE FIBER

**10** When your spinning hand reaches your fiber hand, tighten your spinning fingers and pull the fiber forward.

Remember to relax the hand that is holding the fiber so that it can move smoothly.

By now, you have moved from drafting out the leader and fiber to just drafting out the fiber. You are really spinning!

Can you feel the rhythm now? One hand tightens, and the other loosens. Remember: the sequence is pinch, pull, slide, relax.

## ADD MORE TWIST TO THE SPINDLE

By now, you have probably needed to add more twist to your spindle. The best time to do this is when you have entered the twist all the way up to the fiber hand. Firmly pinch your fiber fingers closed. Reach down with your spinning fingers to give the spindle another twist. Move back up to the fiber hand, tighten your spinning fingers, and relax your fiber fingers. Pull out more fiber, and slide your fingers up the stretched-out fiber. Enter the twist. Keep spinning with this rhythm until the spindle reaches the floor.

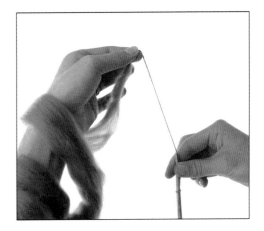

## WIND THE SPUN YARN ONTO THE SPINDLE

When the spindle reaches the floor, it is time to wind the spun yarn onto the spindle.

**1** Wind the fiber that you have just spun onto your fiber hand.

**2** Undo the half-hitch knot on the top of your spindle, unwrap the yarn around the bottom of the spindle, and unwind the yarn.

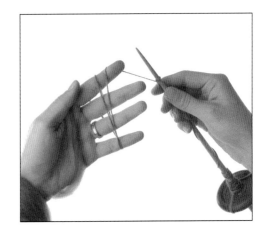

**3** Hold the spindle in your spinning hand.

**4** Twist the spindle to the left. Wrap the yarn from your hand around the spindle. Keep it under tension as you wrap, or it will become a huge tangle.

Wrap two or three times around the base of the spindle, and then wind it part-way up the shaft of the spindle. The trick is to keep as much weight as possible near the whorl.

## CHECK YOUR TWIST

The yarn that you have just spun is called a *single*. This is because it has only one direction of twist in it. To check how much twist your single has, undo a bit of the yarn that is wrapped around the spindle, hang a weight on it, and let it spin back on itself. For the weight, you can make a hook with a little wire and a pretty bead.

### Putting in Less Twist

Too much twist, called *overspinning*, is the most common problem for new spinners. If the single has a high twist, it will be very firm, rough to the touch, and perhaps have little corkscrews of thread showing where the single has twisted back on itself. For some projects, such as novelty yarns and highly energized singles knitting where the high twist is used to contort the fabric, this may be exactly what you need. However, this is generally a sign that you have too much twist in your single.

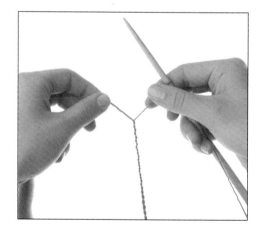

To put less twist in your yarn, you should move your hands a little faster. The more fiber you pull out, the less twist you have in your yarn. Sometimes, your spindle might be too lightweight for the diameter of yarn that you are spinning. Usually, as you fill up the spindle, the extra weight of the yarn takes care of this problem. If that does not help, you can slip a few washers from a hardware store over the spindle shaft to add extra weight.

*CONTINUED ON NEXT PAGE*

## Putting in More Twist

Twist is like a magic glue that holds fiber together. If the single has too little twist, you may have had a difficult time keeping the yarn connected. If the yarn kept breaking and the spindle hit the floor several times while you were spinning, you need to add more twist. To get more twist in the fiber, move your spinning fingers more slowly up the stretched-out fiber. You will feel the twist below your fingers, and you will be able to watch it twist the fiber as it comes up behind your fingers.

Sometimes the problem can be the weight of your spindle. If your spindle is heavy, it can pull the fiber out of your hands too quickly for it to get enough twist. With a heavy spindle, increase the size of the yarn that you are spinning by pulling out more each time you stretch the fiber out.

## WIND OFF YOUR YARN FROM THE SPINDLE

Your spindle is full when the wound yarn is the same diameter as the whorl, or when the weight of the spindle becomes too heavy to spin on. Wind the yarn into a ball that pulls from the center. Place the spindle in a basket or in a box with a hole in it while you wind to keep it from rolling away.

### Wind with a Nøstepinde

1. Hold the nøstepinde in your fiber hand and catch the end of the single under your thumb. (The photo at the right shows a spinner winding a plying ball on a nøstepinde.)

2. With your spinning hand, hold the yarn and wind it toward the left, at a 45-degree angle.

3. As you fill up the space, give the nøstepinde a quarter turn. You will start to cross the threads at a 45-degree angle as you wind.

Using a nøstepinde prevents you from winding the ball too tightly. A tightly wound ball can stretch the yarn and damage its elasticity. You can make a nøstepinde out of dowelling or use a cardboard tube from a roll of paper towels.

### Wind with a Ball Winder

Ball winders are available from knitting and weaving stores. They wind the same type of ball as a nøstepinde, only faster.

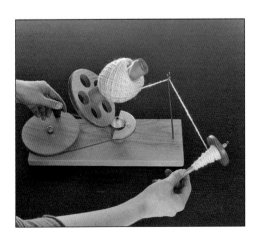

# Spin on a Wheel

Spinning on a wheel is a natural extension of the skills that you learned on a hand spindle. It requires the same hand muscles, and if you have already developed these muscles from using a hand spindle, it should be easier when you add in the treadling movement with your foot.

To begin, you need a wheel, an empty bobbin, 20 inches of two-ply yarn, an orifice hook, and ½ pound of curded roving. Corriedale or a similar type of fleece is a good choice.

## Learn to Treadle

Spinning is an acquired skill. This means that you need slightly different muscles for spinning than you use in daily life. Although you may understand the concept of how to spin perfectly well, it can take a day or two of practice for your muscles to catch up. Be sure to practice turning the spinning wheel consistently before you start spinning.

When treadling, place your foot flat on the treadle. Be careful not to lift your toes or your heel. The following treadle exercises are for both a single and a double treadle.

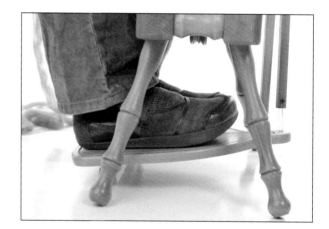

### TREADLE EXERCISES

Start the wheel by pushing firmly on the spokes with your hand. Do not push on the top of the wheel, because this can knock the drive band off.

***CONTINUED ON NEXT PAGE***

## Treadle to the Right

Think of the wheel as the face of a clock. Turn the wheel to the right with your hand. When the footman comes up to the one o'clock position, push the wheel to the right and press down firmly with your foot. Practice treadling this way until the motion feels smooth and predictable. This is the direction used for most spinning. It puts a right-hand twist in the yarn.

If you are using a new wheel, oil it while you are treadling to help the wheel run more smoothly.

## Treadle to the Left

Turn the wheel with your hand until the footman is at eleven o'clock. Give the wheel a push to the left with your hand, and at the same time, press down firmly with your foot. Keep treadling until you can move the wheel smoothly to the left. This direction is used mostly for plying and making novelty yarns.

Practice treadling the wheel to the right again. Switch to the left without using your hands. Although you never need to switch between right and left treadling when you are actually spinning, being able to do so helps you learn to control the wheel.

## TIP

### Find Your Rhythm

You will probably treadle a little too fast when you first start spinning. Most new spinners worry that the wheel will stop if they do not treadle quickly—and it can! However, with practice, you can make the wheel move smoothly.

You should aim for a rate of about 70 turns per minute. Although all wheels treadle a little differently, generally, the bigger the wheel, the slower you have to treadle.

Your hands and feet move in different rhythms when you spin on a wheel; it is like waltzing with your hands and marching with your feet. Your hands move faster than your feet, and so if you treadle too fast, you will have a hard time keeping up with your hands.

## Set Up the Wheel

A spinning wheel is like a musical instrument; it is an extension of your body and needs to be adjusted to you. Every wheel spins differently, even those from the same maker.

As you spin on your wheel, you can adjust it to fit your style of spinning. Remember to make all of the adjustments gently, moving the pegs a fraction of an inch at a time. Keep the wheel spinning while you adjust it, listening to the sounds that the wheel makes, and paying attention to how it feels.

## PUT ON THE DRIVE BAND

### Single Drive

Place the drive band on the whorl (put it on the middle-sized whorl if your wheel has more than one). If the wheel has a scotch brake, make sure that the scotch brake is in place. (The photo at the right shows the spinner moving from the largest whorl to the middle whorl on a three-whorl flyer.)

For bobbin-driven wheels, place the drive band on the bobbin. This type of wheel has a brake on the flyer, and you should make sure that it is in place.

### Double Drive

Place one loop of the drive band over the bobbin and one loop over the whorl. On a double-drive wheel, the flyer whorl must always be larger than the bobbin whorl. If the two whorls are similar in size, the yarn will not wind on the bobbin.

*CONTINUED ON NEXT PAGE*

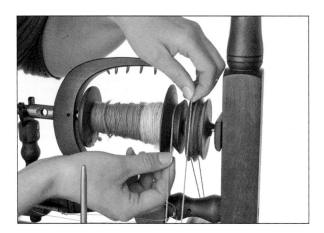

## ADJUST THE DRIVE BAND TENSION

Take all of the tension, including the scotch brake, off the wheel. When you treadle, the wheel should turn while the flyer stays still. Keep tightening the drive band tension until you hear a whooshing sound from the drive band. That is the sound of the drive band skipping. The flyer should start to barely turn; tighten it just until that sound goes away. Do not put more tension on the drive band unless you hear that sound again.

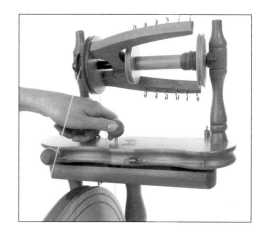

## PUT ON A BOBBIN

The bobbin fits on the shaft of the flyer, and the flyer sits between the maidens, which hold it in place. If you have the wheel-maker's instructions, it should tell you how to replace the bobbin. If you do not have the instructions, every wheel should have some way to take the flyer off so that you can replace the bobbin.

Take the flyer off. If it has whorls screwed to the end of the shaft, take them off as well (a). Slip the bobbin on the shaft, and make sure that it turns easily. Replace the whorls and the flyer. Make sure that the maidens are at right angles to the mother-of-all (b).

Some bobbins are designed to be used with either double-drive or single-drive wheels. They have a groove for the drive band (also called a *whorl*) on either end. One end should have a small whorl, and the other end should have a much bigger one. Remember to put the drive band on the big end of bobbin if you are using a scotch brake, and on the small end if you are using a double drive. The wheel should still work if you put them on the wrong way, but it will not work well.

## ATTACH THE LEADER

The leader is attached to the bobbin with a lark's-head on a bight knot. This simple knot stays tight, no matter which way the wheel turns. Follow these steps to make the lark's-head on a bight knot around the bobbin.

**①** Fold the 20-inch length of yarn in half. Use a plied yarn or the yarn will come apart when the wheel rotates.

**②** Pass it around the bobbin.

**③** Put the loose ends through the loop and tighten.

*CONTINUED ON NEXT PAGE*

④ Loop it again around the bobbin in the opposite direction and pass the loose ends through the loop. Pull tight.

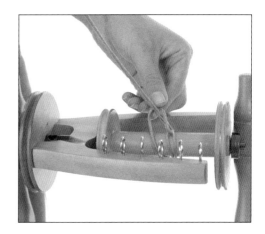

⑤ Thread the leader over the hooks and through the orifice with the orifice hooks.

***Note:*** *You should bend your orifice hook. The curved shape makes it easier to pick up the yarn as it comes through the orifice.*

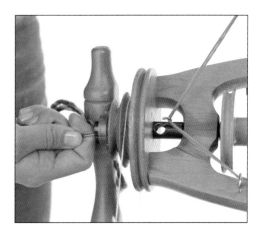

## ADJUST THE BOBBIN TENSION

No matter what type of wheel you are using, there should be a way to tension the bobbin. Tension on the bobbin makes the yarn feed either more quickly or more slowly onto the wheel.

On bobbin-driven wheels like the Louet, the tension can be changed on the bobbin by increasing or decreasing the drive band tension, and the flyer tension gives finer control.

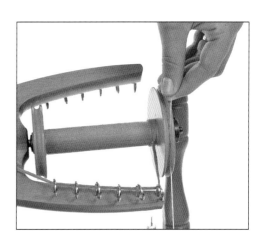

## On a Single Drive

Hold on to the leader with the fiber hand. The spinning hand makes all of the adjustments to the wheel. Now treadle the wheel.

Does the leader pull right out of your hand? If so, then adjust the scotch brake by loosening it. Does the leader feel like you have to push it on the wheel? If so, then adjust the brake by tightening it. Is the drive band making that whooshing sound? Sometimes when you tighten the brake, you also need to slightly tighten the drive band, which can cause this sound—do not do this unless you have to.

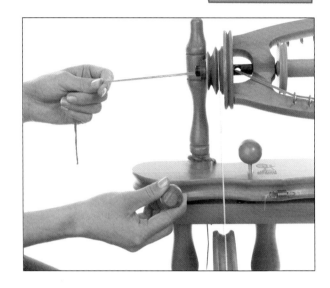

## On a Double Drive

On a double drive, the adjustments for the drive band and the bobbin are made using the same tension device; when you tension one, you tension both of them. Although this is not as precise as the scotch brake, you always have the same ratio between the bobbin and the flyer.

Check your tension the same way as for a single drive (see above). When it feels comfortable for you, it is time to add the fiber and start spinning. You may still need to adjust the tension as you spin, because it will change as the bobbin fills up.

***Note:*** *A good way to remember the tension adjustments is to simply do what the yarn is doing. If it is too tight, tighten the tension; if it is too loose, loosen the tension.*

***CONTINUED ON NEXT PAGE***

## Spin

**1** Lay the leader over the fiber in your fiber hand. With your spinning hand, start the wheel to the right, and push down on the treadle.

**2** Pinch the leader and the fiber with the fingers of your spinning hand and pull about 3 inches forward. Try not to let the twist get into the fiber before you have stretched out the amount that you want.

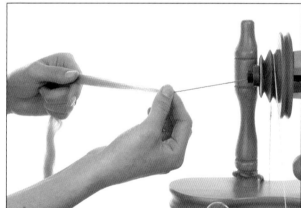

**3** Slide your fingers back to the hand that is holding the fiber. Let the twist from the leader string transfer to the fiber.

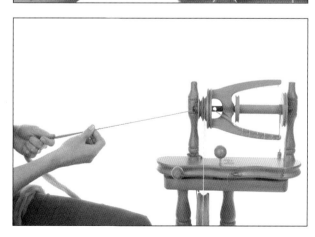

④ Continue with the pinch-pull-and-slide rhythm. You should now be pulling out the fiber by itself, stretching it out, and guiding the twist back to the fiber hand. Remember to relax the fiber hand slightly so the fiber can be pulled out smoothly.

When you run out of fiber, add another piece of roving; use the same method that you used when you transferred the twist from the leader to the fiber. Lay a length of your spun yarn over the fiber and pull a bit of the fiber and the yarn out together. Allow the twist from the yarn to transfer to the fiber.

Now you are spinning!

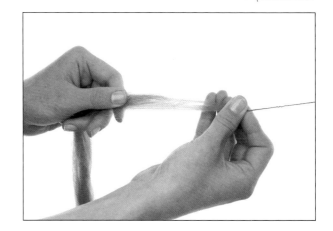

## CHECK YOUR TWIST

Now that you feel comfortable with the basic spinning rhythm, have a look at the yarn that you have made. Pull some of the spun yarn back through the orifice of the wheel. Pull enough yarn back so that you have some of the yarn that was wound onto the bobbin in order to test it.

Use your orifice hook as a weight. Let the yarn spin back on itself, and watch how the hook spins—the faster it twirls, the more twist there is in the yarn. The hook should spin to the right, then to the left, and then it should come to rest. Examine the appearance and feel of this yarn to see if it has the amount of twist that you want.

*CONTINUED ON NEXT PAGE*

**TIP**

**Adjusting Tension**

If you need to adjust the tension on your wheel to get the desired amount of twist, it is best to adjust it while the wheel is spinning. This is because you can feel the changes better when the wheel is in motion.

## Too tight?

Does the yarn look tightly spun, with extra twists of yarn that look like little corkscrews? Does it feel coarser than you thought it would? Is it wiry? If you answer "yes" to any of these questions, then it has too much twist. Spinners call this condition *overspun*.

To avoid overspinning, you should move your hands a little more quickly. Check to make sure that you are not treadling too fast. If this does not correct the problem, then adjust the tension on the wheel. On a single-drive wheel, tighten the scotch brake, and on a double-drive wheel, tighten the tension knob. Remember to make these adjustments gently, a fraction of an inch at a time.

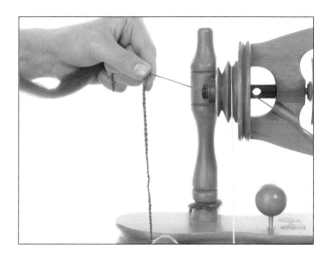

## Too loose?

Does the yarn look wispy? Is it hard to pull off the bobbin, even when all of the tension is released? Is it difficult to join new fiber? Is it too soft to work with? If you answer "yes" to any of these questions, then your yarn has too little twist. Spinners call this condition *underspun*.

To get more twist in your yarn, you should move your hands more slowly. Watch the twist as it comes into the fiber below your fingers, and guide it slowly back to your fiber hand.

You might need to adjust the tension on the wheel. If you have a single-drive wheel, then slightly loosen the tension on the brake. Check to see if the drive band is too tight; loosen it a bit until the wheel does not turn easily, and then tighten it up until the wheel starts to turn comfortably. If you have a double-drive wheel, loosen the tension knob (this loosens both the drive band and the bobbin).

Another cause of underspinning is treadling too slowly. This is unusual for a beginner, but some wheels do need to be treadled a bit faster than others.

## FILL A BOBBIN

As you spin the yarn, it winds on to the bobbin. It then fills up the area directly below the hook that it is passed over.

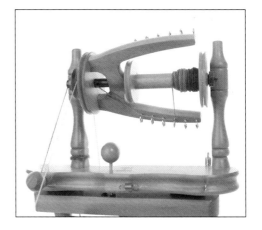

You should move the yarn over the hooks frequently to avoid an uneven buildup of yarn. If you wind it unevenly, this can cause problems later when you ply or wind the yarn off. This buildup can also cause an uneven twist in your yarn.

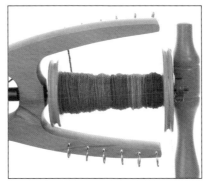

The hooks on most flyers are offset, which makes it easier to fill the bobbins evenly. You move the yarn from the hook on the right side to the hook on the left side, from one end of the flyer to the other.

*CONTINUED ON NEXT PAGE*

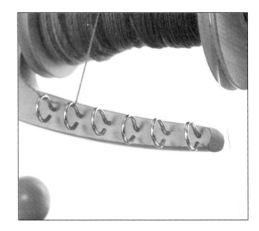

## EMPTY A BOBBIN

Now that you have a full bobbin, you can choose to take it off and use it later to ply with another bobbin (see Chapter 6, "Ply Your Yarn"), or you can wind it off into a skein.

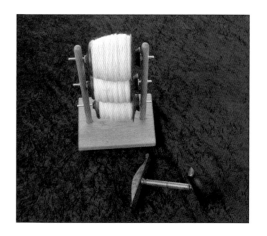

## MAKE A SKEIN

Skeins are a good way to store yarn. They let the yarn relax, they are ready to wash or dye, and you can easily see and feel what the yarn is like. Here is how to make a skein from wheel-spun yarn.

1 Leave the bobbin on the wheel and take the tension off the bobbin.

2 Hold the niddy noddy in your fiber hand and tilt it away from you.

3 Pull a bit of the yarn off the bobbin and tie it to the bottom arm of the niddy noddy.

4 Pass the yarn from the bottom of the niddy noddy to the top in the front.

5 Tilt the niddy noddy toward you and pass the yarn from the top of the niddy noddy to the arm at the back.

6 Tilt the niddy noddy away from you and bring the yarn around the other arm at the top.

7 Come back to the start and continue, making a circle with your yarn until the bobbin is empty.

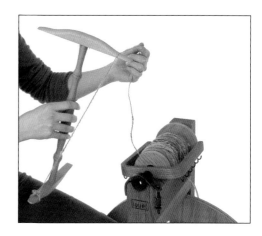

8 Tie off your skein in four places. Use the ends of the yarn for two of the ties, and undyed cotton for the others.

9 Slip the skein off the niddy noddy. Hold it stretched out between your two hands.

10 Twist one hand toward you, and the other hand away from you. Let the fiber relax and twist around itself.

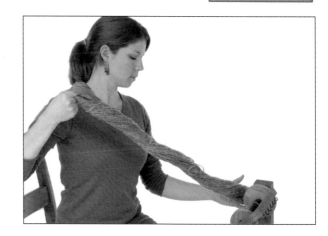

11 Tuck the ends in the skein through one another.

# Troubleshooting

Spinning can give you a lifetime of pleasure, but you are sure to encounter some problems along the way. All of the problems listed here will happen to you at one time or another, as they happen to every spinner. Be calm, take a deep breath, and try one of these solutions.

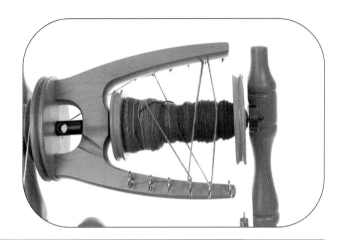

### The wheel is too difficult to treadle.

Check your drive band tension—it should have some give in it. If it is too tight, then try loosening it. See the section "Adjust the Drive Band Tension" on page 70 of this chapter for tips on how to fix this problem. Keep in mind that oiling your wheel can make a huge difference, especially if it is new.

### When I put my foot down, the wheel slides across the floor.

The wheel will slide across the floor if you treadle before the footman reaches the correct position. If you are spinning to the right, make sure the footman is in the one o'clock position—just past the top of the wheel—before you push down on the treadle. If you are spinning to the left, make sure the footman is in the eleven o'clock position when you push down on the treadle. If you treadle when the footman is at the twelve o'clock position, the wheel will lock and you will push it across the floor. Beginning spinners often think that the surface of the floor is too smooth and that the floor is causing the wheel to slide.

### When I push down on the treadle, the wheel flips back and forth.

Check to make sure that your foot is flat on the treadle. When you are just starting to spin, you might lift either your heel or toe. When this happens, it causes the wheel to become unbalanced, and it flips back and forth. If possible, have someone watch you spin, because this is hard to observe by yourself.

### If I tighten the scotch brake enough for my yarn to pull on, the wheel does not turn.

You can tighten the brake to the point where there is so much friction on the bobbin, the wheel cannot turn it and the wheel starts to slip. Try letting off a bit of the brake band tension. If the wheel turns properly and the yarn is pulling in correctly that will solve the problem. If the wheel turns, but the yarn now won't pull on at the speed you need, tighten the tension on the drive band just enough so that the yarn will pull on at the proper speed.

### The yarn keeps getting tangled between the flyer and the bobbin.

This happens because your treadling is not yet even. When the wheel flips right and left, it throws the yarn off the hooks and the yarn becomes tangled between the bobbin and the flyer. Just break it off, hook it up, and start again. Another reason for this may be that the bobbin has become too full, causing the yarn to spill over the edge of the bobbin, and tangle around the shaft.

## I feel like I am going to be dragged into the orifice—I have to hold on to the yarn very tightly.

Try releasing some of the tension on the brake band if it is a single-drive wheel, and off both bands if it is a double-drive wheel. Ensure that you place it on a middle-sized whorl; too big a whorl causes the yarn to pull in very quickly.

## I feel like I am pushing the yarn into the wheel.

First, try tightening the tension on the scotch brake if you use a single-drive wheel, or both the bobbin and the flyer if your wheel is a double-drive wheel. Second, check which whorl you are on; if the whorl is too small, then it puts a lot of twist in the yarn. Sometimes just the friction of the high-twist yarn is enough to stop the wheel from pulling it on to the bobbin. In this case, break it off and start again. Third, check to make sure that your bobbin is not full; this makes it hard to draw on any more yarn. Fourth, check to see whether the yarn is caught around a hook, and that there is nothing to stop it from feeding on to the wheel. Finally, check that the bobbin is moving smoothly on the flyer. Bobbins can swell with changes in humidity, and they can also be made incorrectly.

## I cannot pull out the fiber. It simply will not budge.

Turn the fiber around and try spinning it from the other end. Remember, roving and top both have a right and a wrong end. Also, did you get twist in the fiber? Twist is just like glue, because it is what makes the fibers cling together. Sometimes, no matter how carefully you move your fingers, the twist gets past them. When this happens, the fiber "glues" shut. In this case, stop, pull off a bit of yarn, loosen up the fibers, and start again. If this happens repeatedly, you can try to slightly increase the tension on the scotch brake or the tension on the double-drive band.

## My yarn seems to have a nice twist but when I pull it back, it keeps breaking.

Have you left the brake on? This puts enough pressure on a bobbin that a soft yarn will break when you pull it off.

## I can fill the bobbin up about halfway, but then it does not feed on any more yarn.

As you fill up the bobbin, the dramatic difference between the big circle that the flyer makes and the small circle that the inside of the bobbin makes changes. The fuller the bobbin, the closer in size it becomes to the flyer, and the less the yarn pulls on. In this case, gently tighten the tension on the brake or the tension on the double-drive band as the bobbin fills up to keep the wheel consistently pulling on the yarn.

## I have lost my end!

Take a deep breath, and count to ten. Now roll the bobbin around a few times. Your end is usually under the last hook that it was over—try not to pull until you see the end. You can try a piece of tape to see if it pulls up the loose end; this solution works about half of the time. If not, then pull the most likely end—break it if you have to—and try to pull some of the yarn back. Get enough yarn for a new leader and start again. Keep in mind that it will be a bit messy when you wind it off. Check the tension to make sure that it was not pulling the yarn out of your hands too quickly.

## My yarn seems to be full of lumps and bumps.

Consistent yarn comes with practice; it grows out of the rhythm that your body learns over time. Check to see whether you are pulling out too much fiber. If you are, the yarn will have thick and thin areas, known as *slubs* (see page 90 in Chapter 5, "Types of Spinning"). When you pull out shorter lengths of fiber, the yarn becomes more even. By the time you have spun your first pound of yarn, you will have much more control over the texture.

chapter **5**

# Types of Spinning

Now that you can make a continuous thread, it is time to look at some of the different methods of spinning. In this chapter, you will learn about the two main types of spinning—worsted and woolen. Worsted and woolen are like big families with many relations, and there is a simple way to distinguish these two families from each other: If the twist runs into the fibers after you draft (stretch) them out, then the yarn will be in the worsted family. If the twist runs into the fibers before you draft them out, then the yarn will be in the woolen family. You will learn how to spin both types, as well as why you would choose to spin one over the other.

All of the techniques in this chapter describe different types of drafting. You will learn how to draft your fiber to make slubs and bouclés, and you will also learn how to wash and set the twist on each of these different spinning techniques to bring out their unique characteristics.

**Worsted Spinning** . . . . . . . . . . . . . . . . . . . . . . . . . . . . . . . . . . . .**.84**

**Woolen Spinning** . . . . . . . . . . . . . . . . . . . . . . . . . . . . . . . . . . . . . .**.86**

**Spin a Slub Yarn** . . . . . . . . . . . . . . . . . . . . . . . . . . . . . . . . . . . . .**.90**

**Draft a Bouclé Yarn** . . . . . . . . . . . . . . . . . . . . . . . . . . . . . . . . . .**.91**

**Finish Your Yarn** . . . . . . . . . . . . . . . . . . . . . . . . . . . . . . . . . . . . .**.92**

# Worsted Spinning

In this section, you learn how to choose and prepare fibers for worsted spinning. You learn about the benefits of worsted spinning, and there are step-by-step instructions to help you spin a worsted yarn. Remember, if the twist enters the fibers after you stretch them out, the drafting method is in the worsted family.

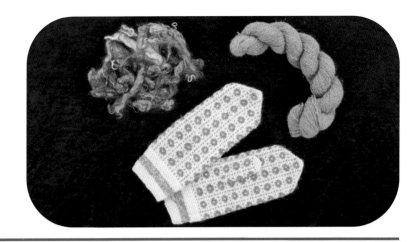

When you spin worsted, you make the yarn smooth, strong, and lustrous. Worsted can withstand abrasion (rubbing), and it sheds water and dirt easily. Because of its strength and smooth surface, worsted is ideal for making socks. It is also the perfect choice for making lace because the clear stitch definition shows the pattern very distinctly. Worsted is also a common method for making warp yarn for weaving.

A worsted yarn is always heavier than other types of yarn because its structure makes it denser and creates fewer air pockets. As a result, worsted yarns produce fabrics that are relatively cooler— whether they are used for sweaters, blankets, or rugs. Because the fibers are stretched and under tension (called *attenuation* in spinning) while they are being firmly spun, worsted yarns also resist felting (the fibers are under tension when the twist enters them and therefore they can't move sideways to lock together).

## FIBERS FOR SPINNING WORSTED

While you can spin almost any fiber worsted, the best fibers for worsted spinning are long, strong, and straight. Fibers should be 3½ inches or longer, and should have less than seven crimps per inch. Lustrous, long wools like Romney, Lincoln, and Cotswold are all good candidates for worsted spinning.

You should always spin silk fiber as worsted because this type of spinning makes the yarn very lustrous.

Flax is another fiber that you should spin as worsted both because of its length and because it is frequently used for a weaving yarn. To make a good warp thread for weaving, you should spin the thread with the twist running into the fibers that are stretched out parallel to one another—this makes them smooth and strong.

## WORSTED FIBER PREPARATION

You can use a worsted method to spin any type of fiber, but to make a true worsted yarn, the fiber must first be put through a special process called *combing*. This process separates all of the short, damaged, and broken fibers from the long, silky fibers. As you learned in Chapter 3, "Spinning Fibers," combed fiber is called *top.*

You can make your own top for spinning by using hand combs. Both the big English combs and the small mini-combs can be used to make top. (For more on worsted fiber preparation, see "Prepare the Fiber" on pages 43–53 in Chapter 3.)

## Spin Worsted

The big difference between spinning worsted and woolen is how you organize the fibers and how you allow the twist to enter them. In worsted spinning, you should make sure that the fibers are as straight and parallel as possible. You should also keep the twist between your spinning fingers and the orifice of the wheel.

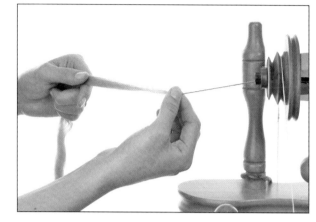

Guide the twist into the stretched-out fibers. Because the fibers are all under tension when the twist locks them in place, they cannot move sideways. This gives worsted its wonderfully smooth and silky surface.

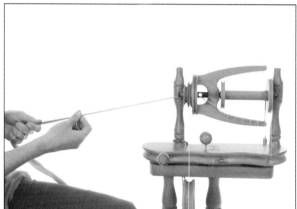

Ply worsted yarns with a firm, balancing twist. A two-ply yarn with the correct twist will be clearly defined—it will look like a string of pearls. A 3-ply ( or more) will be round and have a smooth, even surface. If you have a choice of paired whorls on your spinning wheel, you should spin worsted on the smaller whorl and ply it on the larger whorl. For worsted spinning, you need more twist in the single, and less twist in the ply. For more on plying, see Chapter 6, "Ply Your Yarn."

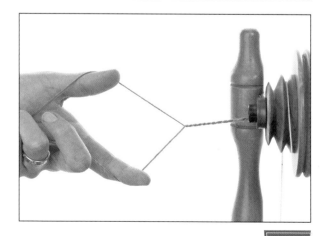

# Woolen Spinning

Woolen spinning produces a very warm and lightweight yarn that has a soft, fuzzy texture. It is not strong enough to be used as a *warp* (threads stretched on a loom) in weaving, but it makes a soft and lightweight *weft* (threads entered between the warp threads). Although it does not withstand abrasion well enough to make good socks, it can make a warm, featherlight scarf. A cashmere sweater is a good example of how you can use a woolen yarn.

## FIBERS FOR WOOLEN SPINNING

You should choose shorter fibers for woolen spinning. These fibers should be 2½ inches or shorter and have a lot of crimp—more than seven per inch. Woolen fibers are very different than those that you would use for worsted. They can be of uneven lengths, and they do not have to be particularly strong.

Bison, cashmere, and yak are all spun woolen, as are Southdown, Dorset, and many merino fleeces. The undercoat of primitive fleeces (page 30) is also perfect for this type of spinning. Angora rabbit is often spun with one of the woolen methods (see page 33).

## WOOLEN FIBER PREPARATION

You usually prepare fiber for woolen spinning using either hand cards or a drum carder. Commercial producers use the same method, but on a much bigger carder. When fiber has been carded rather than combed—as it would be for worsted spinning—it is called *roving*.

In woolen processing, the fiber is opened up and spread into an even batt. This batt is then rolled to help ensure that the fibers are all crossed. For more on woolen fiber preparation, see "Prepare the Fiber" on pages 43–53 in Chapter 3.

## Spin Woolen on a Wheel

Spinning woolen is a little different from the worsted technique that you have learned up to now. Fortunately, it should not be too difficult to transition to woolen spinning because, although you will be moving your hands differently, both hands will still be doing the same work. In woolen spinning, which is often called *long draw spinning*, the fiber hand moves and the spinning hand stays still; however, the spinning hand still controls the amount of twist that is in the yarn.

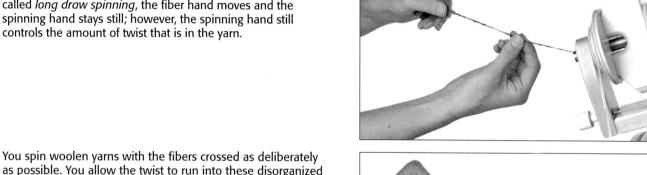

You spin woolen yarns with the fibers crossed as deliberately as possible. You allow the twist to run into these disorganized fibers, and then you stretch out the fibers and add a little more twist. Because most of the twist is running into the fiber without tension, the fibers move sideways in the yarn, creating the fuzzy surface that is unique to woolen yarns.

Your spinning fingers must let go of the fiber to allow the twist to enter the fiber before you stretch it out.

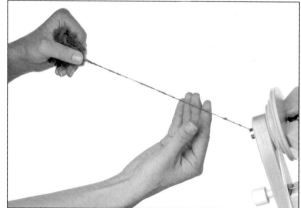

Once the twist is in the fiber, the spinning fingers pinch off the twist and the fiber hand moves back smoothly. When you are spinning, move your hand back as far as you comfortably can; the longer the distance, the more evenly distributed the twist will be.

Woolen should be as light as possible, but if the yarn seems weak and unstable, you should open up the spinning fingers and apply a little more twist. If you plan on using this yarn as a single, then it may need a bit more twist than a plied yarn would require. The extra crimp in the fibers makes the yarn quite a bit stronger than it looks.

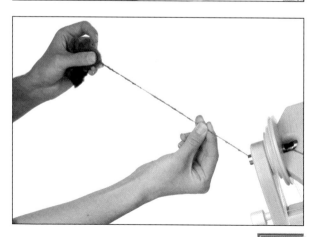

***CONTINUED ON NEXT PAGE***

Once you have as much twist as you need in the fiber and you have pulled it out as far as possible, relax the pressure on the yarn. Let it pull quickly onto the wheel in one graceful swoop.

Leave enough twisted yarn to start the process again. Six inches of yarn should do when you are learning this drafting method; you can shorten it a bit when you feel more comfortable with this new method. Woolen spinning requires a few new muscles, so be patient with yourself.

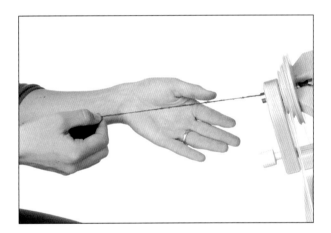

When you spin woolen, the size of the yarn that you make is related to the amount of twist that you allow in the fiber—more twist creates a thicker yarn, and less twist creates a thinner yarn.

Woolen spinning makes a very soft yarn that is mostly air. The single is usually a bit delicate and so it is often plied to give it strength. If you have a wheel that has paired whorls, you should use the larger whorl to spin the woolen single and the smaller whorl to ply the yarn. This keeps the yarn lightweight but strong.

In the single, woolen yarns have a very low twist and are firmly plied. Woolen plied yarn does not show the twist structure. It needs a special finishing technique to make it balanced (see the section "Finish Your Yarn" later in this chapter).

**Note:** *In a balanced yarn, the twist in the single has been perfectly balanced by the reverse twist applied during the plying process.*

## Spin Woolen on a Hand Spindle

Woolen spinning on a hand spindle is called *supported draw*, and it is a great spinning method for short, crimpy fibers such as cotton or dog hair. To start, you should rest your hand spindle on a flat surface—this takes the weight off of the fibers and gives you time to allow the twist to run into them. Once the twist starts to lock the fibers together, it becomes strong enough to *draft,* or stretch, out the fibers. You can use the floor or a bowl to support the spindle (Navajo spinners often use their toes!).

The spindle behaves similar to a child's toy top, and you can use a bowl to keep it in one place. Hold the fiber above the spindle, and allow the twist to run up into the fiber. Pinch the fiber off with your spinning fingers close to the top of the spindle. Draft, or stretch, out the fibers to the diameter that you want. Allow more twist to run in and draft more fiber straight up, and away from the spindle.

Draft the fibers out as far as you can. Just like spinning woolen on a wheel, the amount of twist that you put into the fiber makes it either thicker or thinner. When you have spun as far as you can, wind the fiber around your hand and then wrap it onto the spindle as you would for worsted spinning. There is really no difference between spinning woolen on a hand spindle or on a wheel; they both use the same plying and finishing techniques.

# Spin a Slub Yarn

Slubs are the basis for making many interesting textured yarns. They are simple to make, and as a beginner you have probably made them accidentally many times! Slubs happen when you pull out more fiber than you should; as a result, the yarn has a thin spot on either side of a bump.

You can make slubs easily on either a hand spindle or a wheel. Learning to make a good slub yarn can teach you two useful things: It can show you how to make this classic spinner's mistake into a great design element, and you can learn how to avoid making slubs when you do not want them. Colorful roving—not top—is perfect for your first attempt at creating yarn using this technique. Later, you can try silk and other exotic fibers.

Using the worsted method, pull the fiber with a firm tug. It should pop forward. Just before it breaks, slide your fingers firmly over it, allowing the twist to tighten all of the fibers. Pull again and repeat.

Do you see how the fiber pulls out in even bumps? This is because the length of the fiber regulates the size of the bump.

When you look at your yarn and it has regular bumps, this means that you have been drafting out the fiber too far for even spinning.

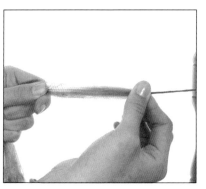 

You can ply slub singles on themselves to make beautiful, strong textured yarn. A two-ply shows the texture most distinctly. You can also ply slubs with a straight yarn for a completely different look. The combinations are really quite endless. You can try both of these plying techniques with your slubs; play with the color combinations and see what you can create.

**Note:** *For more on plying, see Chapter 6, "Ply Your Yarn."*

This drafting technique makes a curly and looped textured yarn. Although it does not create a traditional bouclé, this drafting method produces a similar effect. You can learn about traditional bouclés in Chapter 8, "Spin Novelty Yarns."

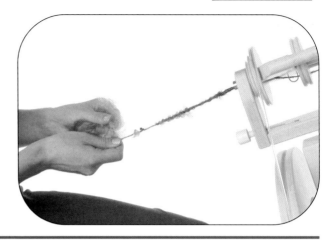

Just like the slub yarn, bouclé yarn is based on a spinner's mistake. When you spin worsted, sometimes a bit of the fiber that you are drafting escapes and is drawn sideways onto the bobbin.

When this happens, it leaves a little curl in what was supposed to be a smooth yarn. For this technique, you should choose fiber that is fairly long and loose. Mohair, Romney, and alpaca all work well.

You can draft a bouclé yarn by making the following mistake on purpose. Use the fiber hand to stretch out a bit of the fiber at a right angle to the fiber that you are drafting with the spinning hand. Relax the sideways fiber so that it wraps around the stretched-out fiber, and then let it go on the wheel. Stretch more fiber out and repeat the process.

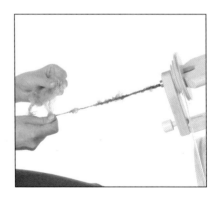

Yarn that you make with this technique is more stable if it is plied. Because you are doing two things at once, it can become a bit over-twisted as a single. Plying takes some of that extra twist out. It also gives you another chance to correct any little wisps that may need to be tucked in.

**Note:** For more on plying, see Chapter 6, "Ply Your Yarn."

# Finish Your Yarn

No matter what type of spinning technique you use and no matter what type of fiber you use to make your yarn, it will need finishing. Finishing allows the yarn to relax and gives the twist a chance to move around and even itself out. For woolen yarns in particular, finishing can also add strength.

## FINISH WORSTED

The simplest way to finish a worsted yarn is to wash it in hot, soapy water, rinse it in clear water, and hang it to dry. You can add an extra rinse with a bit of vinegar or a few drops of an essential oil such as lavender or mint. The vinegar helps to remove any remaining soap residue. The essential oils make it smell nice and may also discourage moths. You should notice that the yarn has much less twist in it once it is washed.

To help the yarn dry more quickly, remove excess water before hanging it to dry. One way is rolling the yarn in a heavy towel and standing on it. You can also use a salad spinner to spin excess water out of skeins and small projects. For larger amounts of fiber or yarn, use a top loading washing machine on the spin cycle. Be sure there is no water coming in on the spin cycle—turn the water off if there is—and add extra towels to increase the amount of water removed.

## FINISH WOOLEN

Woolen yarns need a little extra finishing, called *fulling*, to help them open up. To full a woolen yarn, put the skeins in a bucket of hot, soapy water and pound them with a sink plunger. Rinse the yarn in cold water, and then put it back in the hot water and plunge it again.

Rinse it thoroughly in clear water, and then spin the excess water out (see above). Hold the skein toward the end and smack it against a counter. Turn it around, hold the other end, and give it one more strong smack. This makes the yarn open up and distributes the twist evenly. Woolen yarn has a lot of crossed fibers. When you full it, these fibers move to the outside of the yarn, creating a soft, fuzzy surface.

## WHEN TO FULL YARN

Yarn is fulled after it has been plied and skeined. Generally, all woolen knitting yarns are fulled before you knit with them. Do not full the yarn if you are going to use any of the boiled-wool knitting techniques, such as the processes used for making felted slippers or purses. The process for making boiled wool will full the fabric for you.

Weaving yarns are not usually fulled, either. Instead, the fabric is fulled after it is woven. The fulling process locks the yarns together and makes light, strong fabric that is easy to cut and sew.

Cashmere, bison, and yak yarns change dramatically when they are fulled. Before the yarns spun from these fibers are fulled, they will seem over-twisted and uneven. They will also feel rough to the touch. Once they have gone through the fulling process, the extra twist will be removed and the yarns will become soft and pliable.

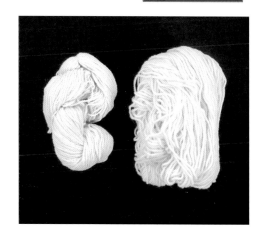

## YARN BLOCKING

Another method of finishing is *blocking*. Blocking is necessary when a yarn has more energy than it needs, which makes the fabric twist out of shape. Blocking can permanently remove the elasticity from yarn, and so you should not block unless you need to.

To start, wash the skein as you would for worsted or woolen. Then stretch it out and let it dry under a bit of tension, such as stretched between two chairs.

If the above method fails to correct the excess twist, try hanging the skein with a bit of weight attached to it. A good method is to hang the damp skein looped over a shower rod. Hang a small weight through it—a damp hand towel will work well—until the skein dries. Usually leaving it overnight will be plenty of time for it to dry.

Slub singles and bouclé yarns often have too much extra twist, which you can release by blocking.

## HELPFUL FINISHING TOOLS

Check the hardware store for inexpensive tools that can make finishing easier. Salad spinners are great for extracting excess water from a skein. A sink plunger helps with fulling by keeping your hands out of hot water. A small, wooden drying rack or a retractable inside clothesline is good for drying skeins.

# 6

# Ply Your Yarn

Now that you have learned the basics of making a single yarn, you are ready to learn how to ply. Plying involves taking two or more threads that you have spun and twisting them together in the opposite direction from which they were originally spun. Plied yarns have an even texture, are stronger, last longer, and resist tangling. They lie smoothly in knitted, crocheted, or woven fabric. Plied yarns are also very efficient. For example, when you choose a plied yarn rather than a single, it will take less yarn by weight to make the same amount of fabric, and the yarns will be much less likely to tangle—a great timesaver. They offer many interesting possibilities, and most designer yarns use plying techniques to create interesting colors and textures.

Why Ply? . . . . . . . . . . . . . . . . . . . . . . . . . . . . . . . . . . . . . . .96

Prepare to Ply . . . . . . . . . . . . . . . . . . . . . . . . . . . . . . . . . .97

Make a Two-Ply . . . . . . . . . . . . . . . . . . . . . . . . . . . . . . . .99

Make a Three-Ply . . . . . . . . . . . . . . . . . . . . . . . . . . . . . .103

Troubleshooting . . . . . . . . . . . . . . . . . . . . . . . . . . . . . . .104

# Why Ply?

Yarns are plied to change what they can do—to give them a more even texture, to make them stronger, and to enable them to wear much longer. Plied yarns also resist tangling and lie smoothly in a finished fabric. A plied yarn is bigger than the singles that were used to make it. Not only is it bigger, but each type of plied yarn works differently when it is used in knitting and weaving.

## Types of Plies

### SINGLES

Because singles have a lot of twist, they often create an uneven and twisted surface that is quite interesting. However, they are not as stable and they do not wear as well as a plied yarn. Singles are also tricky to dye evenly because the surface of a single is hard for water to penetrate, and they tangle easily when you are working with them.

### TWO-PLY

Two-ply yarn resembles a string of pearls. It is much stronger than a single, although it weighs less than a single of the same diameter. The counterbalancing twist of the plying process holds all the singles at rest by the two singles pushing against one another. When this happens, they relax and therefore expand. This is why a plied yarn is efficient; it is bigger and lighter than the combined diameter of the singles held together unplied.

The fiber is protected from wear and light damage when it is plied. Because the two directions of twist balance each other out—think of the singles as hugging one another—a two-ply does not have the wild energy of a single.

Two-plies are traditionally used for weaving. Their corrugated surface locks together to make a strong, lightweight fabric. In knitting, a two-ply does an interesting thing: When you make the knit loop, the loop becomes bigger. As a result, it is the perfect yarn for making lace; it strongly defines the stitches in the lace structure.

### THREE-PLY

There is an interesting difference between a two-ply and a three-ply that makes the three-ply a knitter's best friend: unlike a two-ply, a three-ply has a smooth, round surface. When you use a three-ply for knitting, it does the opposite of a two-ply, by opening up in the knit loop and filling up the stitch. In traditional knitting this is called *blooming in the stitch*, and it means that you are able to use less three-ply than two-ply yarn in a knitting project.

### MULTIPLE PLIES

These yarns have the same characteristics as a three-ply, only more so. They are round, lightweight, and strong. Traditional cable sweaters are made with a five-ply yarn because it shows the surface design so clearly. When you compare a three-ply to a four-ply, you will notice that there is not a dramatic difference in their sizes. The real change is between a single, two-ply, and three-ply.

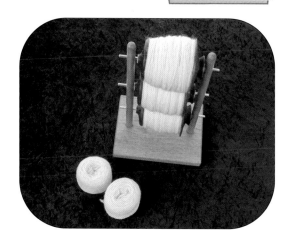

For this task, you need the singles that you have spun, either on two bobbins if you are using a wheel, or rolled into a plying ball if you are using a hand spindle. If your singles are on bobbins, you should use a kate to keep them organized. Many beautiful kates are available, but you can easily make one yourself. If you are going to ply from a ball, you should use a basket or box—even your shoe can work in a pinch—to keep it from rolling away.

## Use a Kate

If you are using a wheel, you need to transfer your singles to a kate before you can ply. You can make the kate that is pictured here using materials that are easily available. You need either a sturdy cardboard box or a small basket, four metal knitting needles, and a handful of cloth-covered hair elastics. Make sure that the knitting needles are the right size to fit through your bobbins.

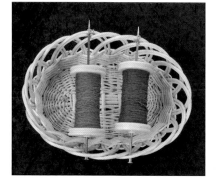
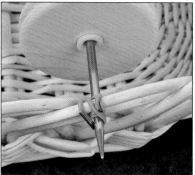

1 Push the knitting needles through the box or the holes in the basket. Try to line the holes up so that the bobbins are straight.

2 Twist the hair elastics over the knitting needles to prevent them from sliding out.

3 Slide the bobbins onto the knitting needles.

4 Secure with the hair elastics.

5 Make sure that the threads are all coming off the bobbins in the same direction, either over the top or from underneath. If they do not pull off in the same direction, they will make a terrible tangle.

**CONTINUED ON NEXT PAGE**

## Make a Plying Ball

If you are using a hand spindle instead of a wheel, you need to make a plying ball to wind the yarn off the spindle. If you do not have a nøstepinde, you can use a paper towel core or dowelling.

***Note:*** *For more on how to use a nøstepinde, see page 66 in Chapter 4, "Start Spinning."*

**1** Take the ends of the two singles that you are going to ply, and tape them together to the top of the nøstepinde, paper towel core, or dowel.

**2** Hold the core in one hand and the joined singles in the other. Wrap the singles on a diagonal around the core so that they lie side by side.

**3** When you have wrapped the singles so that half of the core is covered, give the core a quarter turn and continue wrapping.

**4** Keep turning a quarter turn and wrapping until you come to the end of your singles. If the two balls of singles don't come out evenly, continue to wrap the remaining single around the plying ball in the same pattern.

**5** Tuck the ends of the singles securely in place on the outside of the plying ball.

**6** Unfasten the singles that are taped to the core. Tie a big, obvious knot in them.

**7** Keeping the knot in one hand, slip the ball off of the core.

You now have a plying ball that you can pull easily from the knotted end in the center of the ball.

Now that your singles are either wound into a plying ball (when using a hand spindle) or organized on a kate (when using a wheel), you are ready to ply.

## On a Hand Spindle

1 Put the plying ball in a basket to keep it from rolling away.

2 Tie the two singles to the leader with an overhand knot: Wrap the two ends and the leader around your finger; slip the loop off your finger; pull all the threads through the loop; and pull tight.

3 Hold up the spindle as if you were spinning.

*Note: Remember that a plied yarn is made by spinning the singles together in the opposite direction to the way they were first spun. Your two singles have been created by spinning to the right. To ply them together, you need to twist the spindle so that it turns to the left.*

4 Hold the singles between the thumb and index finger of the fiber hand. Leave about 10 inches of singles between your hand and the spindle.

**CONTINUED ON NEXT PAGE**

⑤ With your spinning hand, reach down and give the spindle a firm twist to the left. Be patient! It may feel like being a beginner again for a little while. You need a few new muscles to twist the spindle to the left easily, but these will develop quickly.

⑥ With your spinning hand, use your thumb and index finger to pinch off the singles about 4 inches from the spindle.

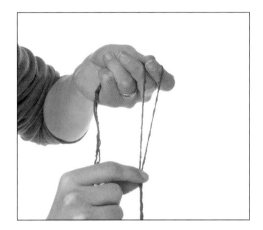

⑦ Let the twist build up behind your fingers, just like you did when you were spinning fiber. When you can feel the twist behind your fingers, move them slowly and evenly up toward the fiber hand. Let the twist follow your fingers like a puppy.

**Note:** *The slower you move your fingers, the more twist the yarn will have; the faster you move your fingers, the less twist it will have.*

⑧ Keep your fingers that are holding the singles gently pinched. The twist should not be able to slip behind these fingers.

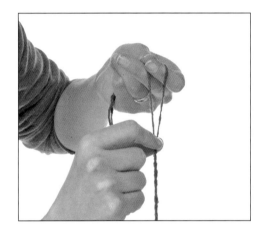

⑨ When your hands meet, pinch off the singles with the spinning hand. Relax the hand that is holding the singles.

⑩ Pull about another foot of fiber out of the plying ball, toward the spindle.

⑪ Reach down and give the spindle another twist.

⑫ Pinch off with your spinning hand until the twist accumulates between your fingers and the spindle.

When you have plied as long a length as you can, wind the plied yarn on to the spindle. Use the same method that you used for winding on the single (see "Make a Plying Ball" earlier in this chapter).

You are now ready to start a new length of plying.

## On a Wheel

Before you start plying on a wheel, you should first practice to ensure that you can make the wheel move easily to the left (see "Learn to Treadle," on pages 67–68 in Chapter 4, "Start Spinning").

**1** Set the wheel up as if you were going to spin. Place the kate on your fiber-hand side.

**2** Pull up the ends of the two singles and attach them to the leader, by separating the leader and inserting the ends of the singles in between.

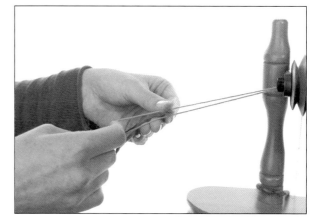

**3** With the palm of your fiber hand facing you, place one single over your thumb and the other over your index finger. Curl your other fingers shut over both of the singles. Try to keep an even tension on both singles.

**4** Start the wheel with your spinning hand, pushing it to the left.

**5** Once you have started the wheel, take the middle finger of your spinning hand and insert it from underneath the V that was formed by the singles that are close to the orifice of the wheel. This separates the two singles and leaves your index finger and thumb free to pinch, pull, and guide the twist up the singles.

**Note:** *If you need to let go with one hand, you should let go with the spinning hand. You will still have the singles in order, as long as you do not let go with the fiber hand.*

**CONTINUED ON NEXT PAGE**

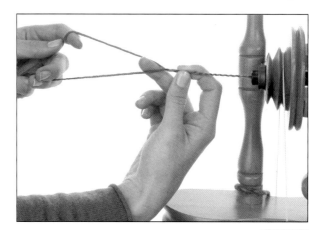

6 Move the spinning hand (here, the left hand) back toward the fiber hand, as evenly as possible. Guide the twist back with your fingers.

7 Use your fingers to smooth out any rough areas.

8 Move your spinning hand all the way back to the fiber hand.

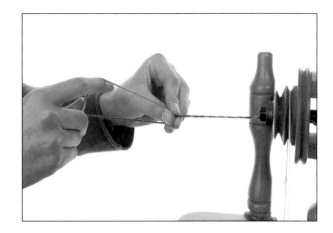

9 Pinch off the singles and pull them forward toward the wheel.

10 Adjust the pressure on the singles in your fiber hand so that the yarns can move smoothly forward.

11 Keep the fiber hand steady. Think of it as being glued in place. If you move this hand, the yarns can lose their tension and become tangled. Moving your fiber hand can also cause the bobbins to jerk back and forth.

When you have fed all of the yarn into the orifice, start the process over again.

## TIP

Make sure the bobbin fills up evenly. Move the yarn from hook to hook more often than you did when you spun the singles. Plying takes a lot less time than spinning.

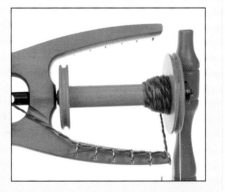

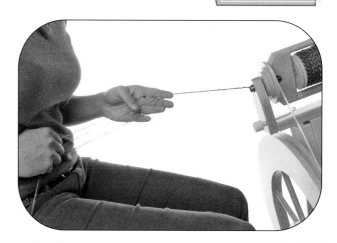

Once you feel comfortable doing a two-ply, you can add in one more single to make a three-ply. If you are plying on a wheel, you should place the extra single over your index finger on your fiber hand. To make a three-ply on a hand spindle, you can make a plying ball as you did with the two-ply, but wind three singles together instead of two.

Remember, to make a plied yarn, the twist must enter all of the singles that make up that yarn at the same time.

## ON A WHEEL

**1** Put the three bobbins on the kate, and place the kate on your fiber side.

**2** Place the three threads across your thigh. With your fiber hand palm down, place your index finger between the first two threads, and place your ring finger between the second and third thread.

**3** Rotate your hand toward your knee; your thumb will slide under the first thread.

**4** Pivot your hand upright. Fold your third and fourth finger over the threads as they come from the bobbins to maintain an even tension.

**5** With your spinning hand palm up, place your middle finger between the first two threads and your fourth finger between the second and third threads. This leaves your index finger and thumb free to guide the twist into the yarn and to make any necessary corrections to the threads.

**6** Start the wheel, just as you did for a two-ply. This time, the plying will be even faster (about thirty percent faster than two-ply). To make sure that the bobbin does not fill up too much in one place, change your hooks often.

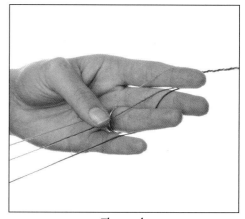

*Three-ply*

## MULTIPLE PLIES

Practice adding singles one at a time until you can do a five-ply. You will notice that each time you add a single, the yarn becomes rounder and more even. There are yarns that have more plies than five, but you must use a special device called a plying template to hold the threads while you ply. Spinners often use a weaver's warping paddle as a template to help separate threads during the plying process.

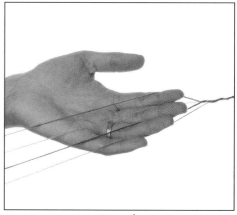

*Four-ply*

Here are some common problems that you may encounter as you ply, along with their solutions.

## What should I do if one of my singles breaks, or if I am at the end of my single and need to start another?

Sooner or later, you are bound to break one of the singles that you are plying. Do not be tempted to tie a knot. You will find that knots always leave a weak spot in the yarn, as well as an unsightly bump. Instead, make a splice by doing the following: Spread the two singles apart; place the new thread between them; start the wheel; and let the twist glue the singles in place.

If you come to the end of the single on one bobbin and have another one to add in, then you can use the same method. It does leave a small area where it has three singles together, but this should not be noticeable.

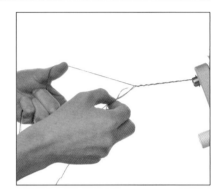

## I am not sure how much ply twist I need.

One reason to ply singles is to produce a balanced yarn (see page 75 in Chapter 4, "Start Spinning"). A balanced yarn hangs straight, and lies evenly in the fabric when it is knit or woven.

Check the twist in your single before you start to ply. Use a hook (see page 75) to see what a balanced ply would look and feel like. Run your fingers over the twist. If you like how it looks and feels, then you should try to create a similar twist when you ply. You should count how many twists it has per inch and measure your plied yarn to ensure that they are similar.

*Balanced*

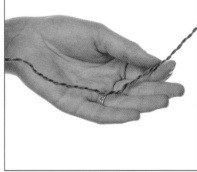

*Unbalanced*

Sometimes the yarn is not quite what you want. You can change it by either adding more twist to the single (spin it again to the right) or removing some of the twist (run it through the wheel to the left). It is the single that controls the balance in a plied yarn.

## I am plying on a wheel; which whorl do I use?

Most spinning wheels come with whorls with two grooves. Traditional spinners use the big groove to spin woolen, and the smaller one to ply woolen. They do the opposite for worsted, spinning on the small groove and plying on the bigger one.

## My plying is uneven.

If your skein seems to have many areas of uneven plying, try counting your foot beats as you spin. This traditional spinning method ensures that you have the same amount of ply twist in each length that you draw out. Count each time that you treadle as you start entering the ply twist. If you get to the fiber hand before you have the same number of twists as the last draw, you should just keep treadling. Feed the yarn into the wheel quickly, using half the number of treadles that you used to draw the yarn out.

This also solves the problem of a skein that is loosely plied at one end—the beginning—and tightly plied at the other end. This problem occurs because the empty bobbin pulls the yarn forward faster than it does when it is full. Counting ensures that the twist is evenly in the yarn before it is wound on the bobbin.

## The woolen that I am plying keeps breaking.

If the woolen that you are plying is constantly breaking, especially if you are using very fine, short fibers such as cashmere or yak, then let it sit on the bobbin for a day or two before you start to ply. It should hold together a lot better.

## My plied yarn is textured with loops and curled edges.

Sometimes the plied yarn can look like it has a curled edge, and even small loops. (This is the way that you would start a bouclé yarn.) This happens when the tension on the singles is not even; if one single is looser, then it wraps around the tighter one. To fix this problem, determine which single is loose and adjust your fingers to put a little more pressure on it.

chapter

**7**

# Make a Cabled Yarn

Now that you know how to ply, you can make cabled yarns. You use the same basic methods as plying, but you add another twist. Cabled yarns are plied yarns that you twist together again, but this time in the opposite direction. When you add this new twist, you create complex surfaces and wonderful color blends, and you make them extra strong as well as beautiful. You can use cables to make everything from a delicate cashmere sweater to a suspension bridge—truly a useful invention.

What Is a Cabled Yarn? . . . . . . . . . . . . . . . . . . . . . . . . . . . . . . . . . . . . . . . .108

Why Cable? . . . . . . . . . . . . . . . . . . . . . . . . . . . . . . . . . . . . . . . . . . . . . . . . . .109

Cable with a Hand Spindle . . . . . . . . . . . . . . . . . . . . . . . . . . . . . . . . . . . .110

Cable with a Spinning Wheel . . . . . . . . . . . . . . . . . . . . . . . . . . . . . . . . . .112

Different Types of Cables . . . . . . . . . . . . . . . . . . . . . . . . . . . . . . . . . . . . .114

Troubleshooting . . . . . . . . . . . . . . . . . . . . . . . . . . . . . . . . . . . . . . . . . . . . .115

# What Is a Cabled Yarn?

When you first look at a cabled yarn, it may look more like a braid or a knitted cord than it does a spun yarn. However, this complicated yarn is actually very simple to make once you understand its structure. In fact, cabling is really just a variation on plying.

To make a cabled yarn, you twist together yarns of two or more plies in the opposite direction of the ply twist. You can classify cables by the number of singles from which they were made. For example, a cable made from two two-ply yarns is called a four-strand cable, while a cable made from two three-ply yarns is called a six-strand cable.

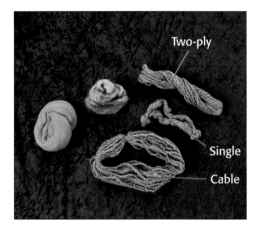

Two-ply

Single

Cable

You can make cables from a wide combination of plied yarns, and they do not need to be used in pairs. For example, you can make an eight-strand cable from a two-ply and a six-ply, four two-plies, or a five-ply and a three-ply. Each combination produces a slightly different surface.

Originally, people used cables because they were a strong yarn. Cables were used for making ropes, such as a cowboy's catch rope, and massive cables made from steel hold up the Golden Gate Bridge.

You can also use cables to make delicate fibers, such as woolen spun cashmere, stronger and more stable.

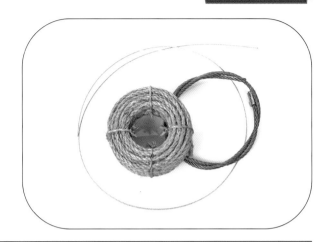

You can use cables to produce yarns with a wide range of textures. You can also cable together plied yarns of different thicknesses or different fibers. The cable shown here is a mixture of handspun linen bouclés and singles combined with commercial two-ply cotton to make the perfect bath-mitt yarn.

You can also use cabling to blend colors; any mix of solid or multi-colored plied yarns can create striking color effects. The yarn shown here is made by cabling together a warm, colored silk slub yarn and a hand-dyed commercial mohair. As you can see, cable variations are endless.

# Cable with a Hand Spindle

Before you start, you need to gather some supplies. You need your hand spindle with a leader attached—use the heaviest spindle that you have. You also need two balls of your handspun two-ply, rolled into two center-pull balls (see "Make a Plying Ball" in Chapter 6). It is also helpful to have a weighted hook, transparent tape, and a handful of brass washers that can fit on your hand spindle.

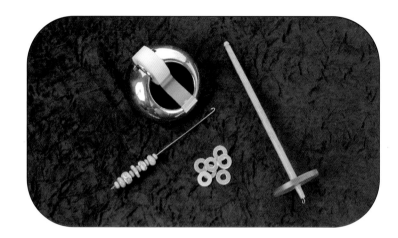

## Re-Ply

The trick to making a yarn cable is simple—it needs to be very over-twisted. By re-plying, you double the twist in your plied yarn.

1 Attach the center-pull end of one of the balls to the leader of your hand spindle.

2 Turn the spindle to the left, in the same direction that you plied the yarn.

3 Use your weighted hook to check the twist. It should fly around as the twist snaps the yarns together.

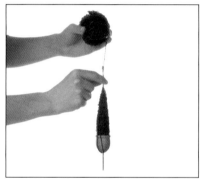

4 Check the yarn sample. It should have a braided surface and hang in a perfect, balanced loop. If it does not do this, you should re-ply it again. It may take several more tries to give the two-ply the twist that it needs to cable.

5 Finish re-plying the two-ply ball.

6 Tie the end of the plied yarn in a knot, and wind it back into a center-pull ball.

7 Tape the end of the yarn to the ball. Be careful not to drop or let go of this end—the twist can run out just like spilt water.

8 Repeat this same process with your second ball of two-ply yarn.

**Note:** To add weight to a hand spindle, slip a few washers over the shaft of the spindle.

## Make a Cable

1. Attach the ends of both balls to the spindle leader with an overhand knot.

2. Hold the yarns in your fiber hand, and pull out a foot of each of the two yarns with your spinning hand.

3. Give the spindle a twist to the right with your spinning hand. Slide your hand back up the yarn to help guide the twist evenly into the yarn. It should take very little time for the two yarns to snap together, as cabling is much faster than plying.

4. Pull out another foot and repeat the same process until you have used up the two balls, stopping to wind the finished cabled yarn onto the spindle shaft when you have reached the length that you can spin. Remember to keep as much weight near the base of the spindle as possible, just as you did when you spun the single or plied your yarn.

5. Wind the yarn into a skein and wash it in hot, soapy water. Depending on the type of yarn and how you are going to use it, you can give it one of the finishes described in the "Finish Your Yarn" section in Chapter 5.

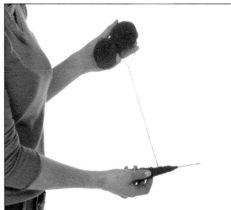

# Cable with a Spinning Wheel

To get started, you need your spinning wheel, of course. Choose the largest whorl pair that you have, and set the wheel up with an empty bobbin that has a leader attached. You need two full bobbins of your handspun two-ply yarn and a kate. Some transparent tape may also be helpful.

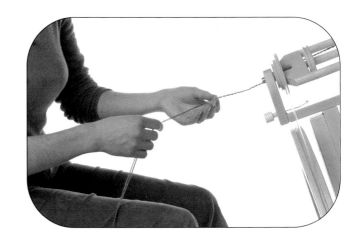

## Re-Ply

1. Place the two full bobbins on the kate.

2. Attach one of the two-plies to the empty bobbin. Re-ply it by turning the wheel to the left; this inserts the extra twist that is necessary to make a cable.

3. Use the orifice hook to ensure that you have enough twist to make a cable. The yarns should snap together, making a new yarn with a braided surface. The yarn should be well balanced and should hang evenly.

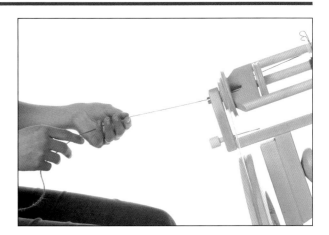

4. If you do not have enough twist, then adjust the wheel so that it does not pull on as quickly. To put in more twist, try a smaller whorl. Check again to make sure that you have enough twist, and continue to re-ply until you have enough twist.

5. When you finish re-plying, you need to secure the end of the overtwisted two-ply. To do this, adhere it to the bobbin with some transparent tape.

6. When this bobbin is finished, place it on the kate. Re-ply the next one, secure it, and then place it on the kate.

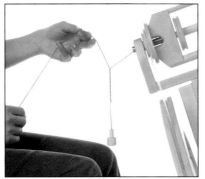

## Make a Cable

1. Set the spinning wheel up using the biggest whorl that you have—these yarns need to pull quickly on the wheel.

2. Take the two ends of the re-plied two-ply and attach them to the leader on your spinning wheel.

3. Spin the wheel to the right to cable. You need to hold your hands a little differently for cabling. When you plied, you kept the yarns separated. This time, just hold them loosely together in your fiber hand. There is no need to guide the twist up as you did in plying; as soon as the yarns touch, they will snap together and form the cable.

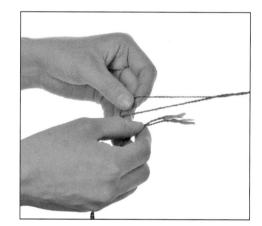

4. The cable should form much faster than the plied yarn did. Make sure that you move your hooks often so that the yarn does not build up unevenly.

5. You might have a little more plied yarn on one bobbin. If there is not more than a foot or two, just fold it back on itself, being careful not to lose the twist. Tuck the end in between the two yarns, and let the twist glue them together.

6. Make sure that the cabled yarn is balanced before you spin too much onto the bobbin. Just pull several feet of yarn back through the orifice. It should hang straight without any tangling. If it is tangled, then read the "Troubleshooting" section at the end of this chapter.

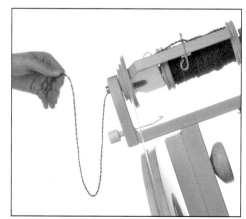

7. When you finish cabling, you can skein off the yarn and wash it in soapy water. Depending on the type of cable, you can apply one of the finishing techniques described in the "Finishing Your Yarn" section in Chapter 5.

# Different Types of Cables

The way that you spun the original single establishes the type of cable that you make. The original twist in the single determines how much twist you need to balance the ply twist—less twist in the single means that you need less to overtwist the plied yarn. The less twist in the yarn, the softer it is; the more twist, the stronger and firmer it is.

Your style of spinning also makes a difference. Worsted spinning produces a firmer, smoother, and more lustrous cable, and the surface shows the sharp definition of the cable twist. Conversely, woolen spinning produces a softer cable. It looks more like a plied yarn, but the fibers are better protected from wear and resist pilling, especially when you have fulled them. (For more on fulling, see "When to Full Yarn" on page 93 in Chapter 5.)

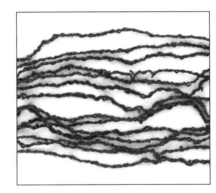

*Woolen*

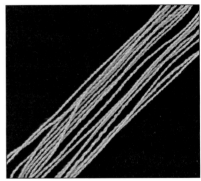

*Worsted*

You can also use commercial yarns to make cables, and it is fun to combine some of the modern novelty yarns with handspun ones. The trick to doing this successfully is to pay attention to how the commercial yarns were spun, and then spin your handspun yarn so that it has the same twist direction as the commercial yarn. You may need to add more twist to make the commercial yarn cable properly. You can do this in the same way that you would add twist to your handspun yarn. The yarn shown here is made with hand-dyed, handspun cashmere that was cabled with a commercial metallic thread that has been plied with a silk/wool blend yarn.

## My yarns are twisted and tangled.

Cabled yarns are a balancing act. In this case, an imbalance has caused the yarns to react with wild energy. When this happens to your cable, trace back the direction of all of the twists that you have made.

A standard cable is made by spinning a single to the right, plying it and re-plying it to the left, and cabling it quickly to the right. It is easy to spin once again to the left out of habit, so check carefully.

If you have made this common mistake, you can just re-cable it in the correct direction. This takes a bit more time, as the wrong twist has to come out before you can enter the correct twist.

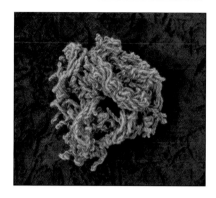

## I do not have enough twist in my plied yarn.

Not enough twist is the most common cause of cabling problems.

You cannot put too much twist in a plied yarn that you are going to cable. To put in such a high twist goes against a spinner's instinct for a balanced yarn, but you need this extreme twist to make a cable work.

Check and recheck to ensure that your plied yarn has enough twist to make a good cable. If it does not, then it is easy to run everything back through the wheel or the spindle in order to increase the twist.

## When I am cabling, the plied yarn does not seem to feed on fast enough.

Be careful to feed the plied yarns on as quickly as possible. You do not need to keep the yarns in order like you do when you are plying. If the wheel does not feel as if it is pulling on fast enough, check the tension. You may need to tighten the drive band on a double-drive wheel. On a single-drive band wheel, tighten the brake first, and then add a little tension on the drive band if it still needs to pull on faster. Check to make sure that you are using the largest whorl that you have.

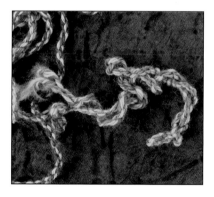

On a hand spindle, cables need a heavy weight to pull on as quickly as possible. If your hand spindle is too light and it is not possible to add weight to it, then roll the yarns on your leg, toward your body (this creates a right-hand twist) and wind them into a ball as they form.

# chapter 8

# Spin Novelty Yarns

Novelty yarns have unusual textured surfaces with strong visual appeal. Because of their textured surface, they can be spaced farther apart in both weaving and knitting. The structure of novelty yarns makes them strong and stable, and they are wonderful yarns for beginning spinners because their uneven surface is very forgiving.

In this chapter, I explain the two key characteristics of novelty yarns—color variation and texture—and how to incorporate unusual drafting techniques, color, and twist to take yarn in a whole new direction. You will learn how to make beautiful color variations using the marled yarn and Navajo ply techniques. I also discuss different types of textured yarns, as well as popular novelty yarns, such as bouclés, garnetted yarns, and encased yarns.

**What Is a Novelty Yarn?** . . . . . . . . . . . . . . . . . . . . . . . . . . . . . . . . . . .118

**Color Variations** . . . . . . . . . . . . . . . . . . . . . . . . . . . . . . . . . . . . . . . . . .119

**Textured Yarns** . . . . . . . . . . . . . . . . . . . . . . . . . . . . . . . . . . . . . . . . . . .124

**Bouclés** . . . . . . . . . . . . . . . . . . . . . . . . . . . . . . . . . . . . . . . . . . . . . . . . . .128

**Garnetted Yarns** . . . . . . . . . . . . . . . . . . . . . . . . . . . . . . . . . . . . . . . . . .133

**Encased Yarns** . . . . . . . . . . . . . . . . . . . . . . . . . . . . . . . . . . . . . . . . . . . .135

Novelty yarns are used everywhere—as feathery winter scarves and gloves, marble-colored wooly socks, sparkling sweaters, and loopy throw rugs. You are not limited to buying novelty yarns in a store; you can spin your own!

Novelty yarns depart from classic spinning, even though most novelty yarns are based on the plying and cabling techniques that you have learned in this book. Rather than the even, predictable surface of classic two-ply, three-ply, and cables, novelty yarns incorporate unusual drafting techniques, color, and twist to take yarn in a whole new direction.

Novelty yarns are a 20th-century contribution to textiles, and they have developed as spinning equipment has evolved. As a result, not all novelty yarns can be spun on hand spindles.

If you are a beginner spinner, you don't need to wait to aquire new skills to make succesful novelty yarns. Often, the uneven texture of a beginner's handspun can be used very effectively to make novelty yarns. The wrapped spiral yarn technique (see "Textured Yarns," later in this chapter) is a good example of a yarn structure that can take uneven and somewhat unstable beginner's spinning and produce a yarn that is both stable and beautiful.

Novelty yarns have another benefit for a beginner. Because most novelty yarns have a textured surface, the inconsistencies that are part of learning to spin become part of the surface design in a sweater or blanket made with a novelty yarn. Many novelty yarns, such as bouclés, also have a structural advantage. The textured surface is designed to hold the fabric together. A garment made from a bouclé yarn will take less stitches than a classic three-ply to make the same amount of fabric, and it will wear very well, looking lovely for years to come.

Color variation is an important feature of novelty yarns. In this section, you learn the two primary color techniques of novelty yarn spinning.

## Make a Marled Yarn

*Marled* colors are solid and swirled, like marble, and this technique produces wonderful color. It is also easy to repeat; as long as you use the same width of colored top and the same color sequence, you will create the same color. You can make enough yarn in the colorway you have designed for any size project—from a pair of socks to a blanket.

To make marled yarn, you need merino top or colored roving in four colors. Although you can make marled yarns from a wide variety of materials, you should make each yarn from the same type of fiber.

**1** Start by holding the fibers side by side in your hand, or put them on mini-combs. If you are using a spindle, diz the colored top off and spin from that.

**2** Hold three pieces of top or roving at a time and spin across the top of the fibers, moving from color to color.

**3** Spin a solid color, then a mixed color, and then a solid color.

**4** When you reach the other side of the fiber, move your spinning hand slowly back to where you began, spinning solid and mixed as you return. If you are only comfortable spinning in one direction, just turn the fiber over and start again.

**Note:** *Remember to check that the fibers are all pulling out in the same direction. Give the fibers a little tug to see which way they pull out the easiest, and spin in that direction.*

**CONTINUED ON NEXT PAGE**

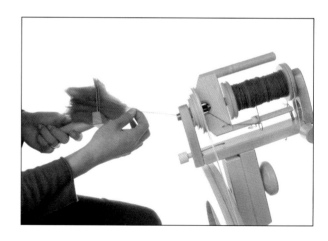

5 Spin across the top of the fibers about 15 times.

6 Rotate the colors by adding the next color on the left side of the fibers, and by dropping the color on the right side.

7 Continue this way, rotating the colors until you have a full bobbin. When this technique is working properly, your bobbin should have blended bands of color across it.

You can use this marled single just as it is for weaving, knitting, and crocheting. You can also ply it in a two-, three-, or multiple-ply, or even cable it. Each time you change the technique, the colors will shift.

Try plying it with a solid color, or use several different color combinations cabled together, such as light and dark or warm and cool.

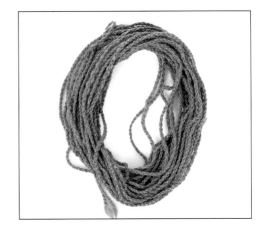

Knit a sample of your marled yarn. The color appears in bands that blend into one another, creating a surface that looks almost airbushed. This yarn was spun from four colors, two-plied, and softly cabled into a four-strand cable. Both the plying and the cabling mix the colors, creating many new color effects.

## Make a Navajo Ply (Chained Ply)

This interesting technique is often used to avoid too much mixing of singles that are spun from multicolored roving or top. Although its origins are unknown, we know that it is a fairly recent addition to spinning in the New World.

Sometimes referred to as a *chained ply,* a Navajo ply is actually not a plied yarn at all, but a chained single that is twisted together. Once it has been twisted, it can be plied or cabled, but it is generally used as a twisted chain.

Although Navajo plied yarn is exceptionally elastic, you should not confuse it with, or substitute it for, a regular three-ply. It cannot level the twist, and each section has one of the lengths of the single lying in the opposite direction. It is perfect for what it does—creating areas of clear color.

To create a Navajo ply, you need to spin a ball or a bobbin of multicolored singles that have sharp color definitions. You can use marling to create the color or spin multicolored roving or top.

*CONTINUED ON NEXT PAGE*

## ON A SPINNING WHEEL

1. Attach the bobbin of multicolored single to the leader. Set the spinning wheel so that it pulls on quickly.

2. Make a loop.

3. Hold the loop with your fiber hand.

4. With your spinning hand, reach through the loop and pull a length through; this forms the next loop. Pull through four or five lengths before you start to spin.

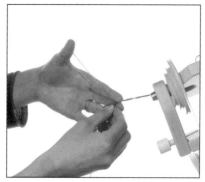
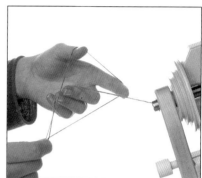

5. Turn the wheel to the left and let the twist tighten the chain that you have made.

6. Continue to pull through loops while the wheel is spinning.

Does this yarn look familiar? It is the same chain stitch that is used to close big bags of flour or pet food. A clever yarn indeed!

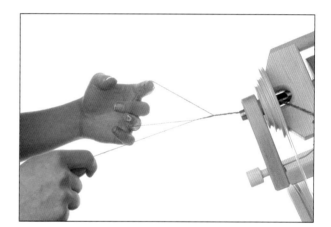

## ON A HAND SPINDLE

1. Choose your heaviest hand spindle or add a few washers (see page 65 in Chapter 4, "Start Spinning").

2. Attach the single to the leader.

3. As in steps 2–4 in the above section "On a Spinning Wheel," make a loop with the single. Pull a few loops through, and hold these with your fiber hand.

4. Reach down and start the spindle spinning to the left.

5. Guide the twist up as you would in regular plying, and wind on each finished length.

## MIX MULTIPLE SINGLES

You can try spinning three different multicolored tops or roving to create unusual color combinations.

Using either a wheel or a hand spindle, attach the three singles to the leader and loop them through, using the same method that you used to create a regular Navajo ply (see the previous page).

## COMBINE TEXTURES

You can try combining textures for another variation on the Navajo ply technique. Choose a variety of textured yarns, using three or four different textured singles at a time. You can mix handspun with commercial yarn and also try different weights. Whatever combination you use, ensure that the last twist on all of them was the same.

Use either a hand spindle or a spinning wheel, and follow the steps for regular Navajo ply (see the previous page). Just like the color variations, you are pulling through more than one yarn at a time.

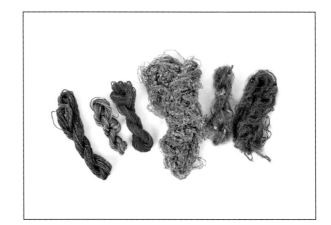

## TIP

When spinning with top, do not strip the top into long lengths before you spin it; this destroys the top formation. However, if it has been dyed, then the top formation has already been changed. Strip it to the right width for the color bands that you want; this makes it easier to spin and it will allow you to control the color intervals.

In addition to color variation, texture is an important part of what makes a yarn a novelty yarn. You can produce an astonishing variety of surfaces by combining different textured yarns together.

## Make Textured Yarns

### SEED YARN

Seed yarn can be made on a hand spindle or a wheel. First, spin two singles—one soft and thick, the other firm and thin. Then simply ply them together. The thin, firm single will cut into the soft one, making little bumps. While this yarn can be made in any combination of singles to produce a wide variety of textures, the strong contrast between the two types of singles will be most effective if you make a two-ply.

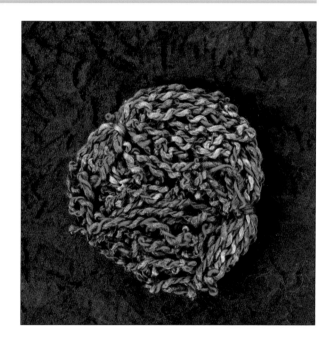

### WRAPPED SPIRAL YARN

You can make wrapped spiral yarn from two bobbins of firmly spun singles. Although you can use different materials and colors for the singles, they should have a similar size and twist.

First, set up your spinning wheel for plying (this particular novelty yarn cannot be made on a hand spindle). Hold one single firmly in your fiber hand, and hold the other one loosely in your spinning hand. As you ply, the loose one will wrap around the tight one. Every 6 to 8 inches, swap the pressure so that the tight one becomes loose and the loose one becomes tight.

## FLAME YARN

Flame yarn uses the same basic technique as seed yarn. However, because it uses slubs instead of even singles, flame yarn is dramatically different.

On a spinning wheel, spin one bobbin or ball of a slub yarn (see "Spin a Slub Yarn," in Chapter 5). Next, spin another bobbin or ball of a finer, even single that has a firm twist. Ply these two together, keeping the tension even on both of them.

To make this yarn on a hand spindle, you need to wind separate balls of the slub and smooth yarn.

## TURKISH KNOT YARN

This technique makes a yarn with beautiful fiber "beads" sprinkled through the yarn. Like many novelty yarns, it is a plying mistake that you make on purpose.

You need two bobbins of singles with a firm twist. They can be of the same material, or you can use a combination of different materials, sizes, and colors.

Keep in mind that because you need two free hands, this is a difficult yarn to create on a hand spindle.

***CONTINUED ON NEXT PAGE***

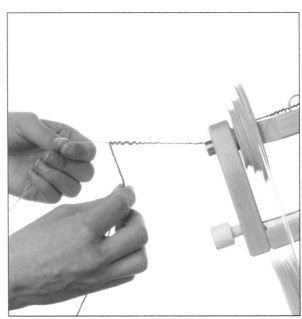

1. Set up your spinning wheel to ply.

2. Hold one single firmly in your fiber hand and the other one loosely in your spinning hand.

3. Pull the single in your spinning hand out at a slight angle to the single in your fiber hand.

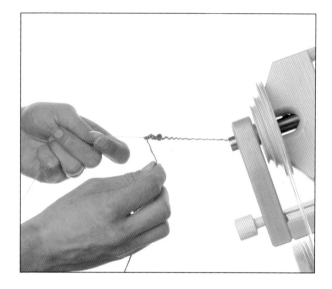

4. Relax the single that you are holding at an angle. Move it up and down the tight single in smaller and smaller lengths, until you build up a little knot.

5. Move the single with which you made the knots back into the regular plying position.

6. Ply a few lengths, and then make your next knot.

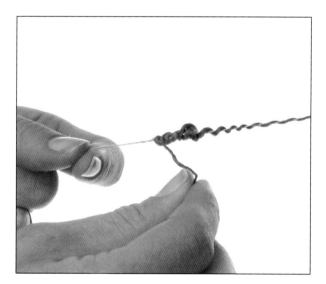

You need to cable Turkish knot yarn either with itself or with another plied yarn to balance the extra twist that develops when you make the knots.

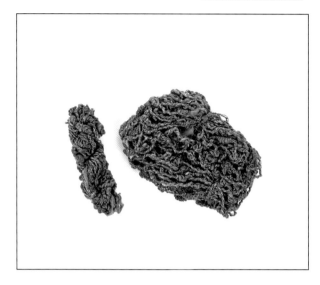

Many novelty yarns are based on an understanding of the direction of the twist on the yarn. To easily discover the last twist given to a yarn, lay the yarn between your fingers and over the palm of your hand. Draw a line across the angle of your thumb to your hand. If the yarn matches the angle of the thumb on your right hand, it has a right twist. If it matches the angle of the thumb on your left hand, it has a left twist.

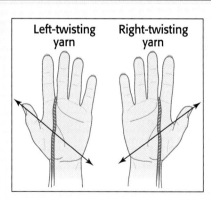

Left-twisting yarn    Right-twisting yarn

# Bouclés

These novelty yarns use twist and unusual drafting techniques to create loops and curls. In fact, *bouclé* comes from a French word that means to buckle or twist.

Although bouclés look as delicate as soap bubbles, they are one of the strongest yarns, and they hold their shape exceptionally well.

You should use long, low-crimp fibers, such as mohair or Romney, to make bouclés. You can use these fibers either unprocessed in locks, or combed into top. Keep in mind that bouclé yarns can only be made on a spinning wheel, not on a hand spindle.

## Make a Mohair Bouclé

The mohair bouclé pictured here is made from kid (baby goat) mohair that has been dyed and spun in the locks. (*Locks* are the naturally occurring divisions in a mohair fleece—just like a lock of human hair.) It was wrapped around a fine, commercially spun cashmere yarn.

To make this yarn, you need a fine commercial two-ply yarn and 2 ounces of dyed kid mohair locks.

1 Tease the mohair locks apart.

2 Set your spinning wheel up with the biggest whorl that you have. This yarn needs to pull on quickly or it will catch in the hooks.

3 Attach the commercial two-ply with an overhand knot.

4 Start the wheel. Turn it to the left.

5 Hold the fiber in your left hand, and use the last three fingers of your spinning hand to hold the yarn. This leaves your index finger and thumb free to help organize the fiber.

***Note:*** *The fiber for this method must be held in the left hand no matter how you normally spin. The yarn will be turning to the left—it won't pick up fiber held in the right hand. In this method, the stretching out of the fiber must be done with the right hand.*

6. Reach over to the fiber with your right hand, and pinch a few fibers with your free index finger and thumb.

7. Move the left hand away, stretching the fibers out at a right angle. The right hand holds the fibers taut.

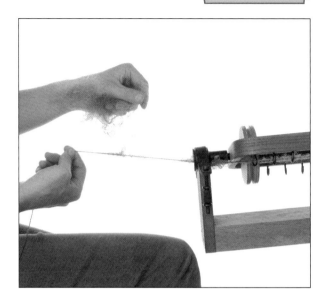

8. Relax the stretched-out fiber, moving it toward the yarn.

9. Keep repeating this motion, allowing the fiber to wrap around the yarn. As the yarn is covered, allow it to feed onto the wheel.

10. If it does not feed onto the wheel, give it a little tug. This should free any of the fibers that may have knotted around the hooks.

11. Fill two bobbins with the mohair bouclé.

**CONTINUED ON NEXT PAGE**

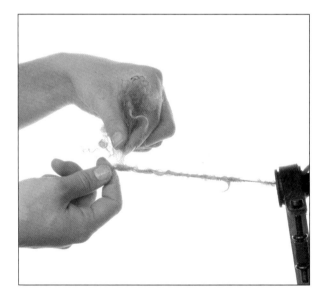

You can now cable these mohair bouclés together to make them stable. Because the two-ply was re-plied when you added the mohair to it, the bouclé should have enough twist to cable easily. Remember to cable quickly to the right.

You can make a variation on this yarn by cabling the bouclé onto a two-ply yarn.

Hold the bouclé out at the same angle as you held the fiber. Hold the yarn firmly. Relax the bouclé onto the yarn, and allow it to feed onto the spinning wheel. Pull out another section of the bouclé and repeat the process.

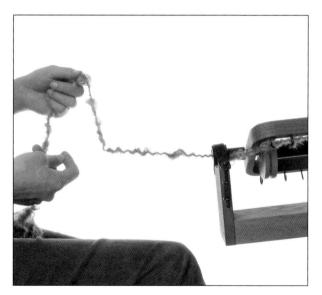

## Make a Silk Bouclé

Many bouclés are created from the tension caused by plying together two yarns that are spun in opposite directions. The easiest way to create a bouclé is to use a two-ply and a single. You should always ply in the direction of the two-ply yarn.

When we put the opposite twists together in this yarn, the fine two-ply becomes even more tightly twisted, and the single unwinds a bit. When they are cabled together, the extreme twist that has built up in the two-ply snaps around the softer yarn, forming it into loops.

Bouclés often use *binder threads* to hold the loop structure in place. These are thin threads that are either loosely cabled with the bouclé as a last step to balance the twist or held tight to increase the definition of the loops. You can use a fine silk, rayon, or cotton sewing thread for a binder. The instructions below will show you how to use a binder thread to define the bouclé's loops.

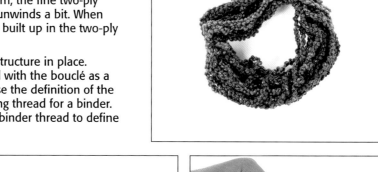

To make this yarn, you need a fine two-ply silk that is firmly spun, and a thicker silk single with a medium twist.

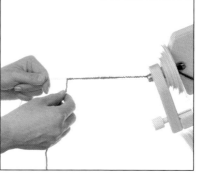

1 Attach the two-ply and the single to the leader on your bobbin.

2 Hold the two-ply firmly in your fiber hand, and hold the silk single in your spinning hand, using less tension.

3 Start the wheel spinning to the left.

4 Relax the silk single so that it wraps around the two-ply. Try to cover the two-ply as much as possible. The loops will not show up strongly until the next step is completed.

5 Fill a bobbin with the wrapped silk and put it on your kate.

6 Attach the wrapped silk and the sewing thread to the leader of the bobbin.

7 Hold the sewing thread tightly with your fiber hand.

8 Turn the wheel to the left again.

9 Hold the wrapped thread at a 90-degree angle, letting it wrap around the sewing thread. As it does, the loops should appear.

10 Fill two bobbins with this loopy yarn.

11 Cable them together quickly to the right.

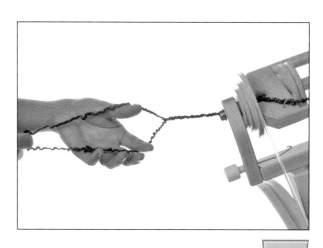

*CONTINUED ON NEXT PAGE*

# Bouclés
## *(continued)*

A push-up bouclé takes a simple bouclé one step further; the softer single is pushed into a loop as the two yarns are plied together.

To make a push-up bouclé, you need one bobbin of singles and a fine commercial two-ply yarn.

**1** Attach the two-ply and the single to the leader on your bobbin. Start the wheel to the left.

**2** Hold both yarns in your fiber hand as if you were going to ply. Use less tension on the single with which you are going to make the loops, and hold the two-ply firmly.

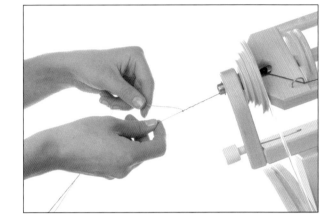

**3** Use the index finger and thumb on your spinning hand to push the loose single into a loop on the two-ply.

The size and the shape of the loops will vary, depending on how much twist there was in the single. The more twist, the crisper and smaller the loop will be. A softer single produces softer and larger loops.

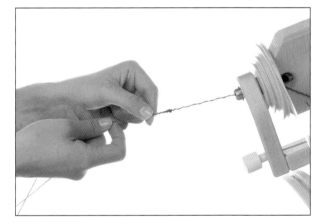

**4** You can bind this yarn with a sewing thread, similar to the silk bouclé, or you can simply cable it back onto itself.

**5** Fill two bobbins with the looped yarn, and cable them quickly to the right.

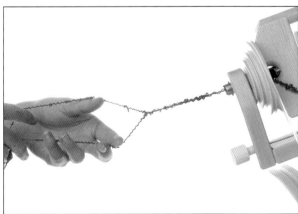

These novelty yarns are made from recycled fabric and threads that are mixed with fiber, carded, and then re-spun. The name *garnetted* comes from the garnet carding cloth that is used in commercial mills to open up recycled fabrics.

Garnetted yarns can be spun on both a hand spindle and a wheel. There is no limit to what you can use: You can experiment with woven and knit materials, leftover yarns, and sewing threads. You can card these materials into any type of fiber.

---

In combinations like the sari silk and llama down shown here, the thread contrasts strongly with the fiber.

To make this yarn, card sari silk waste cut into 3-inch lengths into llama down. Spin a simple, soft, worsted-style yarn and make a two-ply. By using a worsted style of spinning and a two-ply, you bring out the texture of the yarn.

In other garnetted fibers, such as this cotton-and-recycled blue jeans blend that has been done commercially, the individual fibers do not show at all.

***CONTINUED ON NEXT PAGE***

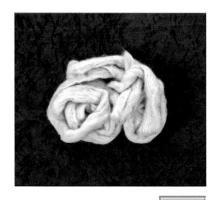

You should spin this fiber using the woolen method. You should also spin it firmly because cotton needs a high twist; it will soften when it is plied. The yarn shown here has been three-plied to make a soft, round knitting yarn.

The yarn shown here is 90-percent recycled-wool-yarn scraps from the historic Pendleton Woolen Mills in Oregon, but any soft, leftover wool yarn will work. To make this yarn, follow these steps:

1 Cut the yarn into 2-inch lengths.

2 Run the wool scraps through a drum carder to open them up.

3 Re-card with a medium-crimp, brown Corriedale fleece.

4 Spin this fiber with a low twist using the woolen method.

5 Either full the yarn before it is used or full the fabric. The sample shown here was knitted and then fulled in the washing machine.

## TIP

The historic Pendleton Woolen Mills in Pendleton, Oregon, has been making fine wool blankets and clothing for more than 100 years. Their signature trade blankets have become collector's items, and you can tour the mill and see fine American wool processed from raw fleece to finished fabric.

# Encased Yarns

Encased yarns have been spun since prehistoric times, when early spinners made yarn with sinew, tufts of rabbit fur, and feathers. Today, we use silk and cashmere to make these novelty yarns, but the technique is the same.

Encased yarns are relatively easy on a wheel, but much more difficult on a hand spindle. These yarns pre-date spindles; where they are still made as ceremonial yarns, they are generally spun by rolling them by hand on the spinner's leg.

To make an encased yarn, you ply two singles together. During the plying process, you insert fabric, feathers, locks of wool, scraps of yarn, and beads between the plies. You then cable the yarn, either back onto itself or with another plied yarn.

1. Prepare the material by cutting or tearing it into 3-inch lengths.
2. Spin two singles firmly using the worsted method.
3. Set these up for plying.
4. Start plying, and insert the fabric at random intervals. They will double up when you ply, and so you should not put them on too thickly.

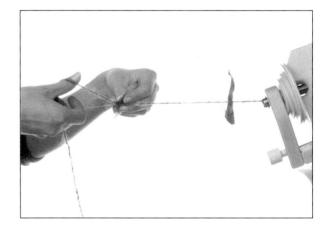

5. Fill two bobbins and cable them together. You can vary this yarn by cabling it with a plain plied yarn. Remember to add extra twist to any plied yarn that you want to use for cabling. These encased yarns have enough twist to cable; the extra twist is added while you are inserting the fabric or other materials.

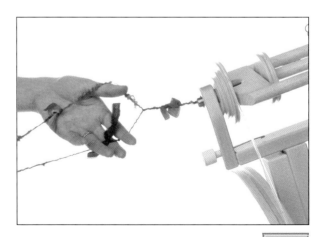

# Spin Exotic Fibers

Have you always wanted to spin silk but just didn't know where to start? Do you have the little bag of qiviut that you received for your birthday still tucked away in your stash? Exotic fibers can be a bit intimidating when you first start spinning, but once you learn a few new techniques for handling them, they are a pleasure to spin.

In order to bring out their special characteristics, most exotic fibers need to be spun a little differently than wool. Most of these methods are based on the woolen and worsted methods that you learned in Chapter 5, "Types of Spinning." Some exotic fibers, such as cashmere and bison, need special finishing to make them stable and strong. In this chapter, you will learn about buying, preparing, spinning, plying, and finishing several exotic fibers.

Alpaca and Llama . . . . . . . . . . . . . . . . . . . . . . . . . . . . . . . . . .138

Angora Rabbit . . . . . . . . . . . . . . . . . . . . . . . . . . . . . . . . . . . . .140

Bast Fibers: Flax, Hemp, and Ramie . . . . . . . . . . . . . . . . . . . .143

Cotton . . . . . . . . . . . . . . . . . . . . . . . . . . . . . . . . . . . . . . . . . .146

Down Fibers: Camel, Dog Hair, and Cashmere . . . . . . . . . . . .148

Goat Fibers: Mohair and Pygora (Type A) . . . . . . . . . . . . . . . .149

Silk: Cultivated, Tussah, and Novelties . . . . . . . . . . . . . . . . . .150

Wild Fibers: Bison and Qiviut . . . . . . . . . . . . . . . . . . . . . . . . .152

# Alpaca and Llama

Alpaca and llama belong to the camelid family. You can spin both of their fibers worsted for a smooth, silky yarn. When you spin them this way, the yarn wears well and has a smooth, lustrous surface. Alpaca fibers in particular need a firm twist to prevent them from stretching out of shape.

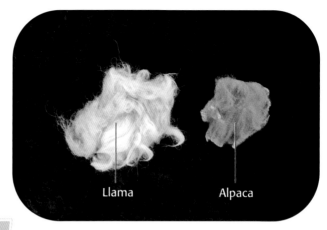

Llama          Alpaca

## Spinning Alpaca and Llama: Over the Fold

For a softer yarn, you must spin alpaca and llama over the fold. This variation on worsted spinning also produces a yarn with a more textured surface.

Yarn that you spin over the fold can be plied easily to make a lovely knitting yarn. You can also use it as a weft yarn in weaving, although it is not strong enough for a warp.

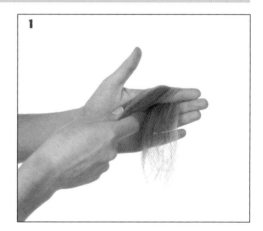

To spin over the fold, follow these steps:

1 First, pull a length of fiber out of the top or use a lock of alpaca or llama. Fold it over the first finger on your fiber hand.

2 Attach the fiber to the leader on the bobbin by placing the leader on top of the fiber.

3 Start the spinning wheel. Let the twist transfer from the leader to the fiber.

4 Pull the fiber over the top of your finger. Let the twist enter the stretched-out fiber.

You finish alpaca and llama as you would finish any worsted spun yarn.

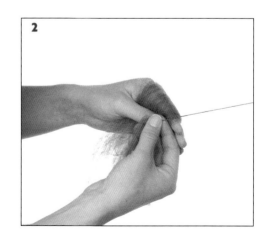

## Dehairing Llama Fiber

Although alpacas have single-coated fleeces, llamas generally have two coats. You can remove the rougher, longer outercoat in a llama fleece by using a pair of mini-combs. The outercoat separates during the combing process, and you can then easily pull it out.

To dehair llama fleece, follow these steps:

**1** Start by placing the llama locks over the combs—with the cut end to the handle of the combs, and the tip end at the front.

**2** Comb through several times. The fiber should separate, with the long outercoat at the front of the combs, and the softer undercoat at the back.

**3** Wrap the long fibers around your finger and pull them out. The soft fiber should be left behind on the comb, ready to spin.

You can spin llama without dehairing if the outer fiber isn't too coarse. It creates a *halo* of fibers around the yarn. (Halo is a term used in the textile world to describe a fuzzy yarn where the fiber surrounds the core of the yarn, like a halo of light around a lamp. Angora and mohair yarns are examples of haloed yarns.)

Angora rabbit yarn creates a soft halo of fiber on the fabric. To bring out this characteristic of the fiber, you need to use a semi-woolen method when spinning. There are three main types of Angora rabbits—English, French, and German Giants—and all three are spun using this method.

## Spinning and Plying Angora Rabbit

### SPINNING

In *semi-woolen spinning*, the twist runs into the fiber. The fiber is then drafted forward as if it were worsted, and a little extra twist is added. Keep your hands a little farther apart than you would if you were spinning worsted, and keep a firm twist on the single.

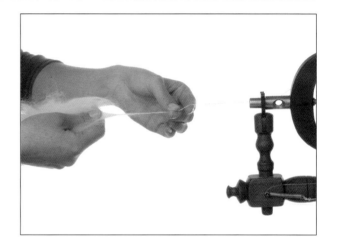

### PLYING

Angora yarn can be used either single or plied. Angora is plied firmly as if it were spun worsted. It loosens up when you ply it, but the yarn does not look fluffy until it is knit or woven. The next step is to finish the skein.

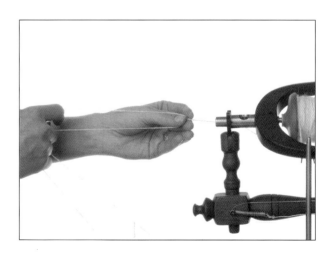

## Finishing Angora Rabbit

Finishing is very important to prevent angora yarns from shedding loose fiber. It also helps to prevent the fiber from felting. The finishing process used for Angora rabbit is called *fulling*.

To full, you need a sink with hot water, detergent, a sink plunger, a bowl of cold water, and a thick towel or salad spinner.

1 Add a squirt of detergent to the hot water, and then add the skein of angora.

2 Use the sink plunger (the water should be too hot for your hands) to agitate the skein.

3 Pull out the skein and put it in the cold water for a few minutes.

4 Return the skein to the hot water and plunge it again.

5 Return the skein to the cold water and rinse well.

6 Extract the extra water by rolling the skein in the towel (a). Press it firmly to remove excess water. If the skein isn't too big, use a salad spinner to extract the water (b).

***CONTINUED ON NEXT PAGE***

**7** Hold the spun angora by the end of the skein. Give it a hard snap against the end of a table or countertop. Turn it around and give it another snap. This opens up all of the fibers that were matted together and helps the yarn to bloom.

Do you see how much bigger the yarn is now that it's fulled? It is also softer and more loosely twisted than it was before.

## FACT

Fulling uses the same techniques as felting—hot water, detergent, and agitation—but the effect is completely different on woolen fibers. Angora opens up and softens instead of hardening and shrinking.

Bast fibers are the skeletal structure of plants, and as a result, these fibers are long, strong, and very straight. Once you get used to their length, they are fun to spin.

You can spin bast fibers either wet or dry. When a bast fiber is spun wet, it activates the pectin that holds the fiber together. Wet-spun yarns are amazingly strong and continue to be strong after they are dry. Dry-spun yarns are softer, weaker, and have a hairy surface.

## Spinning and Plying Bast Fibers

### SPINNING

You must always spin bast fibers worsted because of their length. You need to wrap flax or hemp in a damp towel to help contain the long fibers, while you can spin ramie without the towel because it is a slightly shorter fiber.

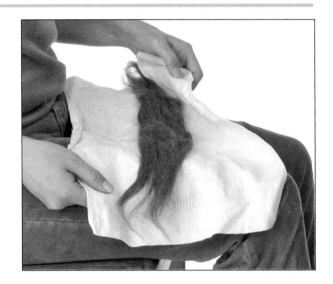

You can wet-spin bast fibers by dipping your thumb in a saucer of water (traditional spinners lick their thumb) just before you guide the twist into the stretched-out fibers.

***CONTINUED ON NEXT PAGE***

# Bast Fibers: Flax, Hemp, and Ramie *(continued)*

## PLYING

Flax, hemp, and ramie are always used as singles unless you have a good reason to ply them. They are the only fibers that can hold a knife-like edge when you iron them, and they also make a smooth, shiny surface. However, if you ply them, you cannot iron them flat.

You should ply or cable bast fibers when strength is more important than a smooth surface. Hemp is used in this example to make a strong, two-ply rug warp.

## Finishing Bast Fibers

You must finish bast fibers differently than animal fibers.

All bast fibers need special finishing because they have a variety of vegetable oils and pectin that need to be removed to make the yarn soft and lightweight. You can remove these oils and pectin by boiling the yarn in water with washing soda and laundry detergent.

1 Add ¼ cup of washing soda to boiling water to ensure that the oils are scoured out.

2 Ensure that there is enough water in the pot to allow the yarn to move easily. Boil for a half-hour. The water should turn the color of tea.

## FAQ

**What is washing soda and where can I buy it?**
Washing soda is a common name for sodium carbonate, and you can find it in the laundry section of your grocery store. In addition to being used in the finishing process of bast fibers, washing soda can be used as a household cleaner, so it's a good item to have on hand. Like its cousin, baking soda, you can also use washing soda to neutralize odors.

③ Rinse the skein under the tap until the water runs clear.

④ Refill the pot with clean water, ¼ cup laundry detergent, and ¼ cup washing soda.

⑤ Boil again for a half hour and rinse.

⑥ Repeat steps 3–5 until the water is fairly clear when the yarn is boiled.

If possible, wash all the yarn for a project together. It will help keep the color consistent.

## Bleaching Bast Fibers

You can safely bleach all bast fibers by washing them in a mixture of water and lemon juice. Use one cup of lemon juice to one quart of water. Soak your skeins in this mixture, and lay them out in sunlight to dry. For best results, lay them out on fresh, green grass. Freshly cut green grass has a very high chlorophyll content. Combined with sunlight and lemon juice, it creates a powerful chemical reaction that very efficiently removes stains, odors and it also bleaches. They still use grass and sunlight industrially in Ireland to bleach linen.

You can also bleach flax and hemp with household bleach. Use ¼ cup of bleach to one gallon of water. Let the yarn sit in this solution for an hour. Rinse well and hang to dry.

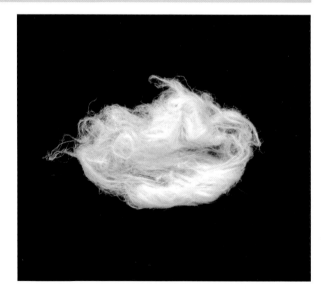

Because cotton is a very short fiber, it can be challenging for a beginning spinner. However, the more prepared it is, the easier it is to spin. You should therefore try spinning cotton top first, and then try loose cotton fiber.

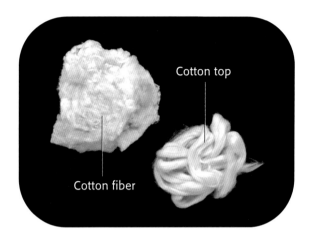

Cotton top

Cotton fiber

## Preparing Cotton Fiber

Cotton is a hollow fiber that has collapsed in on itself. To make it easier to spin, you need to get air back into the fiber by carding it. To do this, you should use cotton hand cards. These are specifically made for carding cotton because they have teeth that are very close together. As a result, the cotton does not pack down between the teeth of the card.

**1** To prepare, catch the fiber on the cards, and then pat it with the top card until it is light and fluffy. Once the cotton fiber is opened up, card it until it is evenly distributed.

**2** Use a knitting needle or a dowel to roll the cotton off of the card. The roll that you make from the card is called a *rolag.*

**3** Tighten the rolag by twisting the stick to the right and tightening the fibers with the fingers of your fiber hand.

**4** Push the fiber up off the stick. When you prepare cotton this way, it is called a *puni.* You can also buy punis ready-made.

Spin from a puni using a woolen draw, just as you would with prepared cotton top.

## Spinning Cotton: The Attenuated Long Draw

You can spin cotton, both top and carded fiber, by using a variation of woolen spinning called the *attenuated long draw*. (Attenuated means stretched out.) In this method, the fiber is drafted back, and an extra twist is added.

1 Draw back as far as is comfortable in a woolen draw (see "Woolen Spinning" in Chapter 5 for a review).

2 Hold the yarn firmly between your fingers. Use your thumbs to add pressure to the yarn.

3 You should feel it slip a bit as the slubs and bumps even out. Give the yarn little tugs until it stops slipping.

4 Use your spinning hand to add twist by rubbing your fingers over any remaining slubs. It is important to keep treadling so that you put enough twist in the cotton.

5 When you have the yarn as even as possible, let it feed on to the wheel and start again.

## Finishing Cotton

Cotton is a vegetable fiber that contains vegetable oils and waxes that you need to remove. You can use the same boiling method to remove these oils as you learned in the section, "Finishing Bast Fibers," on page 144.

Natural colored cottons change color when you boil them with detergent—greens turn blue and browns become darker. These colors will continue to deepen slightly every time you wash them.

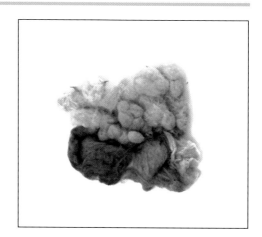

### TIP

Cotton is one of the few fibers that is much easier to spin on a hand spindle. You should use a lightweight hand spindle that puts a high twist in the yarn. If you do not have a hand spindle that is light enough (you can tell because the cotton keeps breaking), use your hand spindle as a supported spindle (see "Spin Woolen on a Hand Spindle" on page 89 in Chapter 5).

# Down Fibers: Camel, Dog Hair, and Cashmere

Down fibers are the fibers in the coats of animals that keep the animals warm in harsh climates. When the weather warms up, this down layer is shed to give the animal a cooler coat. Down fibers have been used to spin luxurious yarns for hundreds of years, and there is nothing softer or warmer.

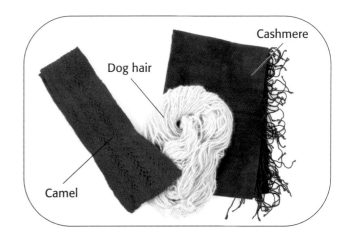

Cashmere

Dog hair

Camel

## Spinning and Finishing Down Fibers

### SPINNING

Camel down, dog hair, and cashmere are all spun using the semi-woolen technique that was described earlier in this chapter to spin Angora rabbit (see page 140). You must keep a firm twist on the single and ply it to make a stable yarn.

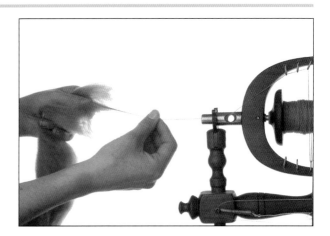

### FINISHING

You must full down fibers in order for them to be stable. Fulling helps these delicate fibers to wear better, and it also prevents the yarn from felting easily. For more on the fulling technique, see the section, "Finishing Angora Rabbit" on page 141 earlier in this chapter. Keep in mind that it is important to full down yarns before you knit with them. Review "Finish Your Yarn" in Chapter 5 for a refresher on how and when to full.

Mohair and pygora type A fibers are long and silky, and they need a worsted draw and a firm twist to keep them from drifting apart. Too often, the type of twist that keeps these yarns stable also tends to turn them into wires that are like stainless steel. To keep the lovely, silky hand (feel) of the fiber in the yarn that you spin, you can use some of the novelty techniques from Chapter 8, "Spin Novelty Yarns."

## Spinning and Plying Goat Fibers

### SPINNING

Mohair and pygora are wonderful fibers for making bouclés, because the yarn structure keeps the softness and the luster intact. Bouclés also make the fibers stable by twisting them in different directions. For more on bouclés, see Chapter 8, pages 128–132.

Spin a bobbin of the fine, tight worsted yarn that keeps the fiber stable, and use it to make a push-up bouclé, as shown here.

### PLYING

Mohair and pygora are strong enough to hold their shape when you use them to make encasement yarns. The firm twist on the two-plied encasement threads locks the fibers in place. For more on encased yarns, see Chapter 8, page 135.

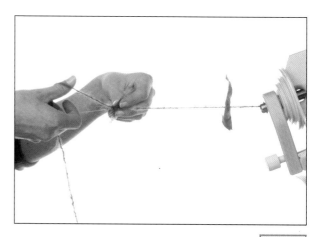

*Pygora goats can produce three different types of fiber: one that is similar to a very fine mohair (type A), one that is a mix of both mohair and cashmere (type B), and one that is similar to cashmere (type C).*

# Silk: Cultivated, Tussah, and Novelties

Silk fibers are triangular in shape, with three flat sides—each as smooth as a mirror. This smoothness makes silk shiny and soft, but to maintain it, you need to take special care while you are spinning. Without enough twist, silk becomes dull and fuzzy and stretches out of shape.

## Buying Packaging

You can purchase silk for spinning in a brick, although the brick needs to be opened up to prepare the fiber for spinning. Start by pulling out the end that has been tucked into the middle of the brick. Because the end is packed in tightly, you need to pull firmly. Shake the length of silk, letting the silk's own weight pull it open. When it is open, pull a length off to spin. Be careful to keep the fibers straight.

Both cultivated silk and tussah are available for handspinning in a top preparation. Just like silk in a brick, cultivated and

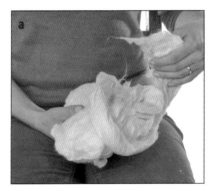

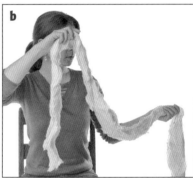

tussah silk top need to be spun with a firm, worsted twist. The less the top is disturbed, the shinier the silk will be. Be careful not to let the twist run into the top when you are spinning, and don't forget to spin across the fibers in a true worsted method. The single will appear quite tight but it will loosen dramatically when it is plied, as there are no scales or crimp structure to hold the twist in place. Ply as you would for any worsted yarn.

Silk is also available in hankies, bells, and caps. These are all basically the same type of silk, but they are processed in different shapes. They are all full cocoons that have been boiled open, turned inside out, and stretched on a frame. Many layers of cocoons are stretched over the frame and then lifted off together to make each hankie, bell, or cap.

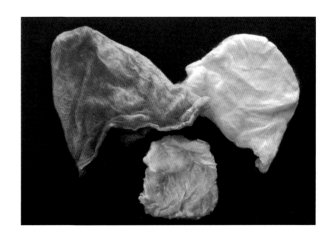

## SEPARATE OUT THE LAYERS

1. Take one edge and quickly pull the cap apart into ten to twelve layers.

2. With both hands, put your fingers in the edge of the cap.

3. Push your hands apart and force the cap to open up.

4. When you have it stretched open as far as possible, start drafting it out.

## DRAFT IT OUT

Take one edge of the hanky or cap and start pulling it out. You should pull it as fine as you want it to spin. This type of silk contains all of the unbroken silk, and some of the fibers are hundreds of yards long. Once you start spinning, you cannot pull the fibers out very much.

## SPIN

Spin with a worsted draw and keep the twist firm. The silk will be very textured with a lot of thick and thin areas, but it will be stable and should wear well.

**Note:** *Be sure to add extra twist to both cultivated and tussah silk. (Check with your weighted hook to ensure that your yarn has enough twist.) Both of these silks should look like a string of pearls when you ply them.*

---

**TIP**

### Handling and Storing Unspun Silk

Unspun silk sticks to almost everything, and so you could end up with more silk on you than on your bobbin. Because silk doesn't stick to silk, you can use a silk scarf to protect both you and the silk. Also remember to push your sleeves up; silk won't stick to your skin, but when you catch silk on your clothes, this pulls the silk out of order and reduces the lovely shine.

To keep the silk in order, you can store the silk that you haven't spun by wrapping it up in a silk scarf.

# Wild Fibers: Bison and Qiviut

Bison and qiviut (the undercoat from musk ox) are rare fibers and are therefore not always available. However, if you can obtain them, you can spin them into the finest, softest, and warmest yarns on earth. Because bison and musk ox live in such extreme climates, they have five different layers of fibers in their coats to protect them from the cold. The fibers that you use for spinning come from the down coat next to the skin.

## Preparing Wild Fibers

Bison and qiviut fibers are commercially available in limited amounts. These fibers have usually been dehaired. However, for fiber that has been hand-collected in the wild and not dehaired, you need to separate out the coarse coats from the down. Follow these steps:

1 First, wash the fiber in hot water and detergent.

2 Rinse it well and let it dry.

Neither bison nor qiviut fibers contain much oil or wax, but both bison and musk ox use mud to protect themselves from insects, and so their fibers may need several washings. The washing process also takes out some of the unwanted coarse fibers.

3 Use mini-combs to separate as many of the long fibers as you can.

4 Push the fiber onto the combs until the combs are half full.

5 Comb through the fiber sideways to separate the different coats.

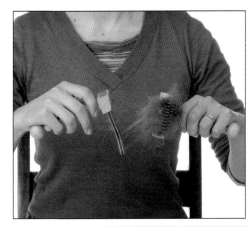

6 Pull the coarse fiber off. Do this several times, separating out the layers of fiber until only the soft, short fibers remain.

7 Diz off the fiber from the combs to spin. You can also spin right off the combs.

**Note:** *These fibers need to be spun fairly fine, so choose a small hole on the diz. Remember that you can always spin finer than the diameter of the hole in the diz, but you can never spin a larger-diameter yarn.*

## Spinning Tips for Wild Fibers

- Bison and qiviut fibers have a lot of crimp. To make the best use of these fibers, you should spin a fine yarn using the semi-woolen technique described earlier in this chapter to spin Angora rabbit (see page 140). This allows the fibers to stay lofty and soft, yet remain strong enough to handle.

- Because bison and qiviut are both very warm fibers, you should spin a thinner yarn so that the clothing that you make with the yarn isn't too hot to wear.

- Spin with a moderate twist, but ply it firmly. These yarns need to be finished using the fulling technique, and a lot of the twist comes out in the fulling process.

- If you are spinning on a wheel, use the smallest whorl you have.

- Keep very little pressure on the wheel when you are spinning these fine yarns. Be patient—you are bound to break the thread from time to time.

- To make sure that you can find your end when spinning these very fine yarns, lay a strip of paper or a stir stick the length of the bobbin every few layers.

- Bison and qiviut can be spun quite well on a hand spindle. Choose the lightest spindle you have. If your spindle is too heavy for these delicate fibers, the thread will break often, making it difficult to spin. If you have difficulty, try using your spindle as a supported spindle (see the "Hand Spindles" section in Chapter 2).

- Full these yarns before you use them unless you plan to weave with them. Bison and qiviut become increasingly fluffy as they are handled.

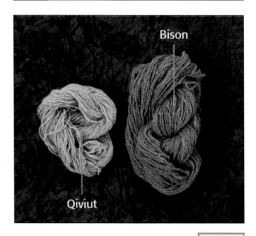

Bison

Qiviut

# chapter 10

# Spin with Color

So far you have learned how spinners use structure and texture to make yarns. Now, let's look at the third aspect of design that spinners use to make yarns that are both individual and beautiful—color. In this chapter, you will learn a number of unusual dye techniques as well as the methods that you can use to spin the resulting yarns. You will also learn how to apply color to fiber and how to blend dyed fibers to create vibrant new colors.

Introduction to Dyes . . . . . . . . . . . . . . . . . . . . . . . . . . . . . . . . .156

Set Up a Dye Space . . . . . . . . . . . . . . . . . . . . . . . . . . . . . . . . . .157

Prepare the Fiber for Dyeing . . . . . . . . . . . . . . . . . . . . . . . . . .158

Color in the Dye Pot . . . . . . . . . . . . . . . . . . . . . . . . . . . . . . . . .159

Novelty Dye Techniques . . . . . . . . . . . . . . . . . . . . . . . . . . . . . .164

Spin for Color  . . . . . . . . . . . . . . . . . . . . . . . . . . . . . . . . . . . . . .166

Spin Carded Color . . . . . . . . . . . . . . . . . . . . . . . . . . . . . . . . . . .168

# Introduction to Dyes

What could be more like magic than dropping a skein of white yarn into a pot and having it come out every color of the rainbow? In this way, dyeing is much more like alchemy than modern chemistry.

There are three main types of dyes that spinners use: weak acid dyes for protein fibers, fiber reactive dyes for cellulose fibers, and nature dyes that dye a range of fiber types. Keep in mind that all dyes, including nature dyes, are chemicals, and that you should use them with care.

## Types of Dyes

### WEAK ACID DYES

Weak acid dyes use vinegar or citric acid to bond the dye and fiber together. They are inexpensive, easy to use, have a low toxicity, and are readily available.

Weak acid dyes are used mainly to dye protein fibers, such as wool, silk, alpaca, dog hair, bison, soy protein, and cashmere. Weak acid dyes also work on bone, shell, plastic made with milk protein (casein), and nylon, which is an imitation of wool protein.

You need to heat weak acid dyes in order for the color to set in the fiber. You can use them as immersion dyes—in a pot of water—or as painted-on and steam-set dyes.

### FIBER REACTIVE DYES

Fiber reactive dyes use soda ash and salt to cause an interaction between the fiber and the dye that melds them together. The best-known and most easily available fiber reactive dye is Procion. This dye has a good color range and is easy to use.

Fiber reactive dyes work on all cellulose fibers, including flax, ramie, hemp, and cotton. They can also dye some synthetics, such as rayon, bamboo, and tencel. In addition, they can be modified to dye protein.

You can use fiber reactive dyes either cold or with heat. Keep in mind that when you use these dyes, you must follow the safety guidelines that come with them.

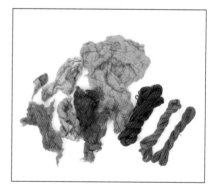

### NATURE DYES

Nature dyes use plants, minerals, and even insects to produce an astonishingly wide range of colors. You can use nature dyes to dye a variety of fibers, including some synthetics. Some dyes need a *mordant*—a chemical salt—to make the dye bond to the fiber.

You can collect plants for dyeing and even grow your own. Commercially prepared extracts are also available, and these give a more predictable color.

There are many good books available to help you learn more about nature dyeing. For some suggested reading, see Appendix A, "The Spinning Community."

A dye space can be as elaborate as a specially built room that includes ventilation and lighting, or as simple as a rollaway cupboard and a hot plate.

## What You Will Need

### DYE POTS

Dye pots need to be big enough so that the amount of material that you want to dye can move freely. These pots need to be inert—stainless steel or heavy enamel. Although you can use aluminum pots, they pit and are hard to clean. (However, these problems won't damage the yarn or affect the color.) You should definitely avoid cast iron, copper, and tin pots because they affect both the color and the yarn. Use separate pots for cooking and dyeing to avoid health risks.

### HEAT AND WATER

In order to dye your material, you need a heat source. For small quantities of material, a crockpot is a simple, inexpensive, and safe way to dye them. A microwave or an electric hot plate can also work.

For dyeing larger amounts of material, a gas barbecue makes a great heat source. It offers good heat control, and gas is inexpensive. Remember that you cannot use portable propane indoors.

You should also have a water source and a drain close by.

### LIGHTING

You should use artificial lighting in your dye space because natural light changes too much to be dependable. An incandescent flood and an overhead florescent produce the perfect light for dyeing. If you need something more portable, Ott-Lite makes several lamps that mimic natural light.

### OTHER HELPFUL DYEING TOOLS

Here are some other items to help you keep things clean and organized when you dye:

- Sticks and large wooden or stainless-steel spoons to stir and lift the skeins from the pots.
- Strainers of any size and material to drain wet fleece and strain natural dye baths.
- Plastic pails with handles to soak fiber and skeins before dyeing or washing.
- Plastic tablecloths to help protect against spills.
- Old towels, blankets, and lingerie bags to help with washing and rinsing skeins and fiber. Lingerie bags keep fibers contained during the washing process. Layer the towels and blankets in your washing machine to help absorb the excess water.
- Portable, folding, drying racks to dry yarn. A towel between the racks is good for drying fleece.
- A small postal or kitchen scale to weigh dye powders and plant material, as well as the fiber that you want to dye.
- Paper towels, a few sponges, a roll of plastic wrap, and a box of freezer-weight plastic storage bags. Wrap skeins and fiber in plastic wrap or place them in plastic storage bags to dye in a microwave.

# Prepare the Fiber for Dyeing

Before it can be dyed, fiber needs to be scoured to remove all of the grease and oils. (See pages 144–145 in Chapter 9, "Spin Exotic Fibers," for more on how to scour.) Dyes are carried by water, and so even if you have purchased your fibers and yarn clean, they need to be soaked thoroughly in order for the dye to take evenly.

## TIE THE SKEINS

Tie each skein in four places with undyed cotton yarn and a loop of cotton sheeting (strips of a cotton bedsheet will work) to prevent the yarn from slipping out of the individual skeins. Tie loosely—the yarn and the ties will become bigger as they absorb the water.

Tight ties leave a repeatable mark where the dye couldn't penetrate the yarn. This interesting dye effect looks better when it is done on purpose than by accident. It is called *ikat*, and is used by dyers all over the world.

## SOAK

You can soak raw fiber just as it is, or you can place it in a netted bag to keep it contained. You should tie roving loosely with strips of cotton sheeting to make it easier to move it.

To soak the raw fiber, fill a bucket with warm water and a bit of detergent—1 tablespoon to a gallon. Let the yarn or fiber soak for at least a half-hour, and longer if the fiber is very fine, like cashmere, silk, or cotton.

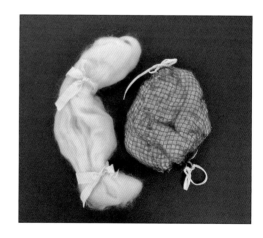

# Color in the Dye Pot

You can apply dyes to fiber in many different ways. For example, you can dye raw fiber, top or roving, yarn in various stages, and fabric after it is knit or woven. You can dye perfectly even color or deliberately uneven color, and you can also produce random or repeatable colors. It's your choice and, like cooking, which it closely resembles, it's all a question of doing it to your own taste.

## Use Weak Acid Dyes for Protein

You need to follow the manufacturer's instructions for mixing up the dyes. After you have mixed your weak acid dyes, they will keep indefinitely in a stock solution.

There is no relationship between the amount of dye and the amount of water in a weak acid dye bath. The relationship is between the dye and the fiber, and so you'll get the same color in a cup of water as you would in a gallon.

Weak acid dyes use household vinegar, citric acid crystals, or ammonia sulfate to help the dye bond to the protein. It is added to the dye bath before the fiber is entered.

### DYEING FIBER

Use caution when working with all dyes, even nature dyes. Avoid unnecessary exposure to the powder. Use gloves, and wipe up spills. If you weigh out powder, use a mask.

Measure the vinegar and dye into the dye pot. Stir well. If you are dyeing fiber, place it straight into the pot. Slowly bring the dye bath to a boil. Don't stir, as this can cause felting.

Lift the fiber out of the dye bath from time to time. Let the dye run back into the pot, and then place the fiber back into the dye bath.

*CONTINUED ON NEXT PAGE*

## DYEING SKEINS

You must dye skeins on a rod over the pot. Rotate the skeins through the dye bath to allow the dye to penetrate evenly. Bring the pot up to a simmer. When you have the color that you want, drop the skeins into the pot and turn the heat off.

Let your skeins or fiber cool in the dye bath. Dyes adhere by molecular motion—there is as much motion when the dyes cool as when they heat up.

Rinse in soap and water to remove any dye that has not stuck to the fiber. Rinse in a mild (¼ cup to a gallon) vinegar bath, and hang to dry.

## Use Fiber Reactive Dyes for Cellulose

When working with fiber reactive dyes, you must follow the manufacturer's instructions. Read the safety guidelines carefully. Wear the correct mask to weigh out the dye powder. Measure everything out, including the fiber that you want to dye. Weigh out the fiber dry, and record its weight. Make sure that the fiber to be dyed is well scoured and completely wetted before placing it in the dye bath.

When dyeing cellulose fibers, you need to carefully measure out the water using the dye instructions. You also need to measure out the salt in proportion to the weight of fiber that is to be dyed. The deeper the color you want, the more salt you need to use.

This dye bath cannot become any hotter than 100 degrees, and you can use any container that will tolerate that temperature.

The slower you add the soda ash, the more even the dye bath will be. Because cellulose fibers won't felt, you can stir often—the more you stir this dye bath, the better.

After the cellulose fiber is dyed, it needs one more step. When it comes out of the dye bath, it needs to go into a bath of hot water and laundry detergent. Bring the pot to a boil for 15 minutes. Don't omit this step because it's an important part of the dye process.

Because you will have dye left in a fiber reactive dye bath, it's very important to wash the finished yarns. Rinse, rinse, and rinse again—the more water in which you can submerge your fiber, the better. This ensures that the dye will not run.

When rinsed thoroughly, fiber reactive dyes are lightfast and washfast, which means that they won't fade. They produce rich, jewel-like colors on both fiber and yarns.

*Note: Fiber reactive dyes can only be mixed up as needed. They do not keep in a permanent stock solution.*

**CONTINUED ON NEXT PAGE**

## TIP

### Dispose of the Dye Bath

With practice, you will have no dye left in the dye bath. However, the first few times, you will probably have dye left over because you may have put too much dye in the pot. You can store leftover weak acid dye and nature dye and use them again, but you should dispose of other leftover dye baths. If you have to dispose of a dye bath, it is safe to pour weak acid and fiber reactive dyes down the drain, as they won't harm sewers or septic fields. You can neutralize fiber-reactive and acid dyes by adding vinegar or baking soda, respectively. Nature dyes in large amounts should be poured over soil, not poured into a septic field.

## Nature Dyes

Nature dyes use the chemicals found in plants, minerals, and some insects to make color. Many nature-dye recipes go back thousands of years. Using nature dyes connects us to our history.

When you create color with plants, you can make a full spectrum of beautiful colors. Plant material can be collected and used either fresh or dried, and the range of materials that you can use is endless.

Most nature-dye material is first made into a dye liquor. You must crush the plant material and put it in an inert pot, preferably stainless steel. Simmer for an hour, and then strain off the liquid. Add this liquid to the dye pot if you are ready to dye. However, if you aren't going to use it right away, you can store it in glass canning jars. (It will seal if you pack it hot and use a canning lid.)

Many nature-dyed colors use chemical salts called *mordants*, which you add directly to the dye bath, to make the nature dyes bond to the fiber. Yarns can also be pre-mordanted, dried, and stored ready for future use.

Because some mordants are toxic, you should handle them carefully; wear a mask and gloves when weighing them out. You can mix mordants up in a liquid solution and store them in glass jars to be used as needed. Many mordants use another chemical, such as acetic acid or cream of tartar, to help the fiber absorb them better.

Add the mordant to the dye bath or add mordanted skeins. Heat to a simmer and stir gently. You should start to see color in the first half-hour.

You can obtain interesting colors by using one mordant in the dye bath, and then placing the yarn in an after-bath of a different mordant.

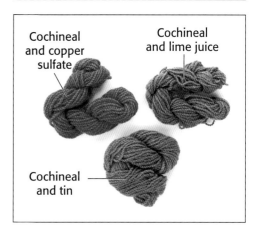

Cochineal and copper sulfate

Cochineal and lime juice

Cochineal and tin

## NATURE'S COLOR PALLET

All of the colors shown here come from just a few natural dye materials: indigo, cochineal, black tea, and lichen. The mordants are alum and lime juice. Both are nontoxic and easy to use.

*Indigo* is a fermentation bath that is made from a number of different plants that contain a chemical called indicafloria. You can buy indigo ready to use. Cochineal is a little insect from South America. The lichen used is *Letheria vulpina*, which is found in pine woods. The tea is common black tea.

The skeins were dyed in this order:

- Lichen over white wool
- Lichen over gray wool
- Lichen, cochineal over white wool
- Cochineal, lime juice, alum over white wool
- Cochineal, lime juice, alum over gray wool
- Cochineal, lime juice, alum, indigo over white wool
- Cochineal, tea over white wool
- Cochineal, tea over gray wool
- Indigo, cochineal, lichen over gray wool
- Indigo, cochineal over gray wool
- Indigo, cochineal, tea over gray wool
- Indigo, lichen over gray wool
- Indigo, tea over white wool
- Indigo over gray wool
- Indigo over white wool

**Note:** *There is an excellent new indigo on the market. It's called freeze-dried and it is as easy to use as instant coffee.*

# Novelty Dye Techniques

You can use a dye pot to create unusual color effects. When dyeing your fibers, be playful with color, and don't stop until you have the color that you like. Remember, your mistakes can be corrected, everything can be dyed again, and the more you dye, the easier it becomes. The methods shown here are fun, and will help you to learn how dyes work.

## RAINBOW POT

You can use a crockpot for this colorful dye bath. Follow these steps:

1. Put 2 inches of water and ¼ cup white vinegar in the crockpot. Turn up the heat to high.

2. Pack wet, washed fleece in the pot. Make sure that the pot is packed so that the fiber can't move freely.

3. Follow the dye instructions for mixing up a stock solution of weak acid dyes—one of yellow, one of magenta, and one of turquoise or cyan.

4. Imagine the pot being divided into three triangles. Then pour one dye solution into each triangle. They will run into one another, creating new colors where they overlap.

5. Put on the lid, and let the pot heat up. Check every half-hour to see if the dye is absorbed. Allow the fiber to cool in the dye pot, and then rinse and dry.

## PAINTED ROVING

You can use this method with either fiber reactive dyes or acid dyes. If you are dyeing cellulose, then soak the roving in soda ash and use fiber reactive dyes. If you are dyeing protein, then soak the roving in a strong vinegar solution—1 cup per gallon of water—and use acid dyes.

You need a microwave or a double boiler to heat the roving. You also need 4 ounces of roving, dye in powder form, plastic cups, several natural bristle brushes, plastic wrap, vinegar, and rubber gloves. Follow these steps:

1. Stretch out enough plastic wrap to hold the roving. Lay the roving on the plastic wrap, coiled or looped to fit.

2. Mix the dyes in plastic cups, ⅛ teaspoon dye powder to ¼ cup water.

3. Use the brushes to apply the dye, like paint.

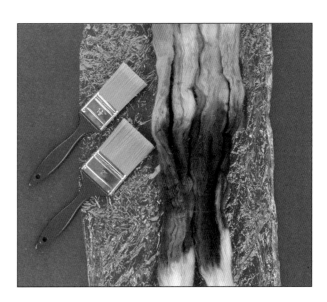

④ Roll the roving in the plastic wrap for protein fibers. Steam for 45 minutes or use a microwave (see below). Make sure that the temperature reaches 185 degrees Fahrenheit. If you have a temperature probe, you can use this to check the temperature of the roving. Cellulose fibers don't need heat; let them sit in the wrap for 24 hours.

**Steam your roving to set the dye:** Place it in the top of a double boiler. Add water to the bottom of the double boiler. Bring it to a simmer. Place the top part of the double boiler on the bottom. Put a lid on the double boiler. Let the pot simmer for 45 minutes. Do not open the plastic-wrapped roving until the roving has cooled.

**Use a microwave to set the protein dye:** Place the plastic-wrapped roving in the microwave. Turn the microwave on medium heat for 3 minutes. Check the roving; it should be quite hot to the touch. Let it cool. Use a paper towel to check it for excess dye. If dye comes off when the roving is patted with a paper towel, put it back in the microwave on medium heat for another 3 minutes. Repeat this process until dye no longer comes off on the towel.

⑤ Let it cool slowly to room temperature in the plastic wrap. Unwrap it and rinse out the excess dye. Rinse cellulose fibers especially well.

## MULTICOLORED BALLS (FOR PROTEIN FIBER ONLY)

This method uses the yarn itself as a resist, to tie-dye the yarn into dots of color. This yarn is fun to knit or weave, and is also perfect for making many of the novelty yarns that are discussed in Chapter 8, "Spin Novelty Yarns." You can use this method to dye either singles or plied yarns. Follow these steps:

① Roll the yarn into loose balls.

② Pack the balls dry into a crockpot. They need to fit snugly.

③ Fill the crockpot with water until the water just covers the balls.

④ Add ½ cup vinegar. Let this soak into the balls, and then turn the crockpot on high.

⑤ Add the dry dye to the balls using a chopstick. Stick the chopstick in the dye powder and then poke it down between the balls, changing colors often. Use the chopstick to add some dye to the top of the balls as well.

⑥ Let the dye bath come to a simmer. Simmer for a half-hour, and then allow it to cool.

⑦ You may find some places where the dye didn't penetrate. Return these balls to the crockpot and add a bit more dye to them.

⑧ Rinse, squeeze them out, and let them dry.

# Spin for Color

You can use the novelty techniques in this section to spin the fibers that you have dyed. This brings out the beauty of the colorful fibers.

## Color Techniques

### SPIN A RAINBOW

You can make this yarn from mohair locks dyed in a rainbow pot. You need to organize the locks into color groups that duplicate the color in the pot. Follow these steps:

1. Lightly loosen the locks.

2. Pick a fine wool or silk commercial two-ply.

3. Attach the two-ply to the leader on your spinning wheel. If possible, you should use a large whorl on the spinning wheel. If you don't have a large whorl, then you can tighten the drive band a bit.

4. Start the wheel to the left. Hold your loosened mohair locks in your left hand.

5. As the two-ply yarn's twist tightens, the locks are caught into the yarn. Let the yarn pull quickly onto the wheel, catching the locks as it goes. Use your right hand to pull the fiber apart a bit. Try to keep it at a right angle to the plied yarn.

6. Choose the locks in the color sequence that you have laid out.

7. Fill a bobbin.

8. Bind the single by putting the full bobbin on a kate. Attach the single and the two-ply to the leader.

9. Quickly cable these two yarns to the right.

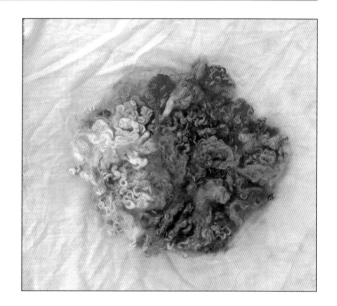

## SPIN A PAINTED SKEIN

There are endless ways to spin the beautiful colors that you can create by making painted rovings. One of the most popular ways is to use the Navajo, or chained ply, method (see page 121 in Chapter 8, "Spin Novelty Yarns"). This technique keeps the colors from becoming too blended in the plying. Another effective way to use painted singles is to ply them with a solid-colored single.

For both of these methods, the color patterns are more striking if you split the roving into smaller widths before you spin. Usually, you would avoid splitting roving or top because it pulls the fibers out of order. It also loosens the fibers and makes them a little harder to spin consistently. Roving that has been dyed has usually floated out of order in the dye bath. No matter how carefully it is handled, most dyed roving and top becomes more compact, and even a little felted. Pulling it apart helps to make it easier to spin.

## PLY FROM PAINTED BALLS

Tired of just plying white yarn? You can ply from these painted singles and treat the singles like paint. You can dye a range of color systems and ply them together in as many combinations as you like. Try different plies—two, three, or four. Because the angle of the yarn changes with the number of plies that you use, the colors that you create will change with every ply. Don't forget to try cables with these yarns as well. You can also ply yarn from painted balls with a solid.

You can use yarn from painted balls to make novelty yarns. Try them with Turkish Knots (page 125) and the push-up loop bouclé (page 132).

# Spin Carded Color

You can produce yarn with vibrant depths of color by carding dyed fiber. You need a selection of dyed fibers, either hand dyed or commercially dyed, and a drum carder or hand cards.

Start with strong colors to ensure that you still have lively colors by the time they are knit or woven. Bright colors might seem garish on their own, but as you blend colors together on the carder, they will lose some of their harshness. They continue to blend as you spin, and blend even further as you ply.

You can use a color wheel to help you design interesting color combinations. This color system uses the complementary colors orange and blue, using one-third orange and two-thirds blue, carded three times through a drum carder.

This color system uses a split complement: two-thirds violet and a one-third mix of blue-green and gold.

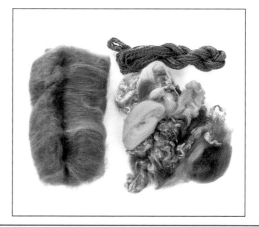

This is an analogous color system, meaning that all of the colors (blue, yellow, and green) are next to each other on the color wheel. It has been carded three times through the drum carder.

This is a monochromatic color system, meaning that there is only one color. The variations come from adding white, gray, brown, and black. These variations are added by weight, one-third of the variation to two-thirds magenta. When white is added, it creates a tint; gray creates a cool tone; brown creates a warm tone; and black creates a shade.

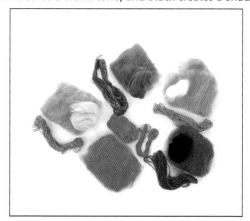

## Plying for Color

You can create an endless range of colors using solid-colored singles that are plied together. This technique is more effective if you use a three- or four-ply because the color shifts are subtler. Keep in mind that you should try to keep the colors close to one another.

These samples were created in commercially dyed merino that was spun worsted and then three-plied. To ply for color, follow these steps:

① Spin three half bobbins of your first color. (In the sample, this color is blue violet.) Make a half bobbin of three-ply, solid color.

② Spin three half bobbins of your second color. (In the sample, this color is teal.)

③ Ply two strands of your first color with one of the second.

④ Ply two strands of the second color with one of the first.

⑤ Ply three strands of the second color.

⑥ Continue adding in new colors.

### TIP

Out of bobbins? You can wind some of your yarn into balls. You can also spin on top of any leftover yarn—there is bound to be some left on the bobbins. At the end of your project, you can ply any leftovers together to create an interesting tweed yarn.

# chapter 11

# Use Your Handspun

What could be better than using your own yarn to knit or weave? Whether it's a sweater for yourself or a colorful pair of socks for a friend, working with the yarn that you have created from start to finish is very satisfying. You can use the information in this chapter to help you plan out knitting projects, adapt your yarn to commercial knitting patterns, or design patterns of your own. You will also learn how to make a simple loom, as well as the basics of weaving with your handspun.

**Knit with Handspun** . . . . . . . . . . . . . . . . . . . . . . . . . . . . . . . . .172

**Weave with Handspun** . . . . . . . . . . . . . . . . . . . . . . . . . . . . . . . .178

# Knit with Handspun

Knitting with yarn that you have spun yourself is a special pleasure. Whether you decide to use a commercial knitting pattern or design a project yourself, here are some tools and ideas to help you get started.

## Make a Swatch

Before you start a knitting project using your handspun, you should make a sample swatch. This helps you to learn what your yarn will look like and feel like when you knit it into fabric. Knitting a swatch also helps you to figure out your *gauge*—the number of stitches per inch and the number of rows per inch in knitted fabric.

Yarn can be full of surprises. Whether you use a pattern that already exists, or design something of your own, it is a good idea to make a swatch or even a series of swatches. A good swatch is a wonderful road map that makes everything flow smoothly.

To begin, gather up a selection of knitting needles, a tape measure, a knitting needle gauge, some straight pins, and the handspun yarn with which you want to knit. You also need a steam iron and a cloth to press your sample.

### FIND THE RIGHT NEEDLES

Take a length of your handspun, fold it in half, and slip it through the holes on the needle gauge. Check the needle size on the hole that it moves through best. It should move through easily, but not have a lot of extra space.

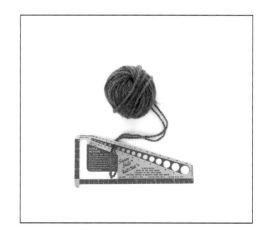

## KNIT THE SWATCH

Knit your first swatch with the knitting needles that you have selected. Cast on twenty stitches, and then knit twenty rows. Knit using a stockinette stitch (knit one row, and then purl one row), or use the stitch pattern that you are planning to use for your project.

Knitting is very individual. A needle that is the right size for another knitter is not necessarily right for you. The swatches shown here are knitted from the same yarn on three different sets of needles. After knitting this first swatch, knit a second one using needles that are one size larger. Then knit a third swatch with needles that are one size smaller.

**Note:** *If you are using textured or uneven yarn, you will have a more accurate sample gauge if you make a bigger swatch. Try knitting a 10×10-inch sample.*

### Check Your Knitted Fabric

Lay your swatches on a flat surface, and lightly steam them with a steam iron. Use a cloth to cover each swatch as you press it. Let them lay flat until they are cool. Don't block it with pins—later, when you measure the swatch, you want to measure its natural size.

To assess your swatches, ask yourself: How do they look? Rub them with your fingers. Does the knitted fabric feel good? Does it hold its shape?

You should also consider how this yarn would work in the project that you have in mind. Different kinds of knitting projects need different types of yarn. For example, a yarn that is smooth and strong enough to make a pair of comfortable, long-wearing socks might not be the perfect yarn to make a delicate, lightweight scarf.

Now study the swatch. Is the knitting straight? Sometimes knitted fabric twists in a bias and does not lie flat. This is caused by the yarn having too much twist for the size of the needles that you are using. Try needles that are a size smaller. You don't want to create a bias because it does not iron or block out.

If the yarn is still twisting out of shape, change the pattern that you are knitting. A moss or a seed stitch usually corrects the bias. If this doesn't work, try blocking your yarn before knitting. To do this, wash the yarn in warm, soapy water and then rinse it in clear water. Hang it up wet to dry with a light weight on it. A washcloth through the loop of the skein works well as a weight.

***CONTINUED ON NEXT PAGE***

A good way to check a yarn's ability to wear well is to use it to knit a cuff. Wear the cuff for a few weeks. If your handspun is going to stretch out of shape or *pill* (creating little bumps of broken fiber that felt on the surface of knitted fabric), then these problems will show up in the cuff.

## Figure Your Gauge

After you check your fabric and select which swatch you want to follow, place the swatch on a flat surface.

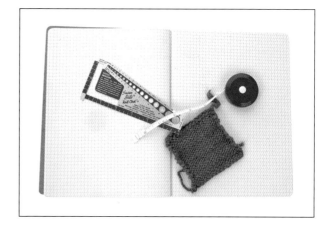

Use a needle gauge or a tape measure to count the number of rows per inch in your swatch. Take the measurements toward the center of the swatch. Measure 2 inches, count the rows, and divide by two. This should give you a more accurate measurement than just measuring 1 inch. Be as accurate as you can, and don't round the number off.

Calculate the number of stitches per inch in the same way. Measure 2 inches, and divide this number by two. Again, don't round off. Calculate to a quarter of a stitch.

Write down the number of rows per inch and the number of stitches per inch. These numbers can help you when you design your knitting project (see "Design Your Own Pattern" on page 177).

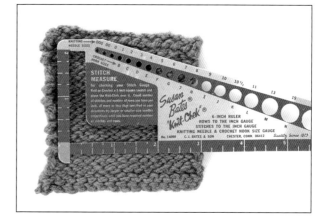

### USE A MCMORRAN BALANCE

A *McMorran balance* is a simple, inexpensive tool that measures how many yards there are in a pound of yarn. It is available in most weaving supply stores. You can use it to calculate how many yards of handspun you have.

Many knitting patterns help you to understand how to substitute yarns by giving you the yards per pound for the yarn that they have chosen for the pattern. Along with your sample swatch, this measurement can help you to figure out how your yarn will work in a commercial knitting pattern.

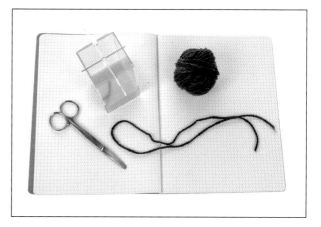

1 Place a length of handspun yarn over the balance beam.

2 Cut off small bits of the yarn until the balance beam becomes level.

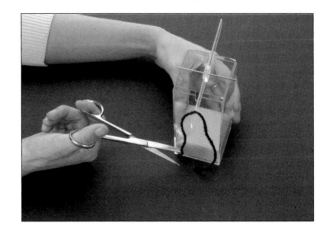

3 Take this length of yarn and measure it with a tape measure. Be careful not to stretch it.

4 Multiply the yarn measurement from step 3 by 100. This will give you the number of yards in a pound of your handspun yarn.

If your yarn has a lot of texture or an uneven surface, you should take three measurements, add these measurements together, and then divide by three. This gives you an average for the yards per pound and is more accurate for this type of yarn.

**CONTINUED ON NEXT PAGE**

## Choose a Pattern

Once you have figured out the right gauge for your handspun, it's time to choose a pattern. You can use a commercial pattern or create a pattern of your own.

### USE A COMMERCIAL PATTERN

You should look for a commercial pattern that uses a yarn similar to your handspun. If possible, look at a ball of the commercial yarn that the pattern is using.

Check the gauge and compare it with the gauge from your swatch. Count both the stitches per inch and the rows.

Most packaged yarns give you the number of yards in the skein. Multiply the number of yards out to a pound and check it against the yards per pound in your handspun (see "Use a McMorran Balance" on the previous page for how to calculate yards per pound).

If the yarn used in the pattern and your handspun are the same yardage and the gauge is similar, then you will be able to use your yarn with the commercial pattern without adjusting the pattern.

### Adjust a Commercial Pattern

The yarn that you want to use will usually not be quite the same as the commercial yarn. It's always easier to adjust the pattern to your yarn rather than adjust your yarn to the pattern. Trying to force your handspun into a gauge that is too tight or too loose can take away much of the beauty of the yarn.

Most patterns include a drawing of the garment, showing the measurements. You should make a list of these measurements, and use them with your stitch gauge to calculate how many stitches you need to cast on and how many rows you need to knit. Check as you knit to make sure that your knitting is still within the measurements of the pattern.

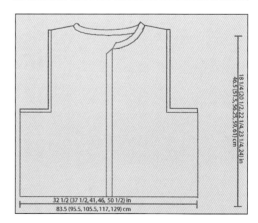

For Shetland jacket —

2 ply shetland spun
from Gates of the Mountain
Shetland top —

From swatch —
    20 stitches — 4.5 in × 4 in

Vest ? — needs approx. 700 yds
            2 ply

18 1/4 (20 1/2, 22 1/4, 23 1/4, 24) in
46.5 (51.5, 56.25, 59) cm

32 1/2 (37 1/2, 41, 46, 50 1/2) in
83.5 (95.5, 105.5, 117, 129) cm

## DESIGN YOUR OWN PATTERN

The easiest way to begin designing your own pattern is to find a garment with a shape that you like and that fits you well. You should start with something simple, such as a favorite sweater or sweatshirt, and use this as a guide. Take the measurements from this garment and, with the information from your swatch, calculate how many stitches you need to cast on and how many rows you need to knit.

You can figure out parts of the pattern, such as the increase for the sleeves, by measuring the length of a sleeve. Begin by calculating the number of rows that it will take to knit that length, based on the figures from your swatch. Then measure the width of the top of the sleeve and of the wrist. Figure out how many stitches you need to increase from the wrist to the top of the sleeve, and then distribute these increases evenly from wrist to top of sleeve.

You can also use sewing patterns to make a knitting pattern. You should choose a pattern that has simple lines and no complex shaping. You can easily adjust sewing patterns to your size; just follow the directions that come with the pattern. Once you have the pattern pieces adjusted to your size, you can use your swatch gauge to find out how many stitches to cast on. Lay your knitting on the pattern and knit to the shape of the pattern. Decrease and increase as the shape of the pattern indicates.

Looms can be the size of a house or as simple as a wooden frame. In this section, you learn about two types of looms, each of which works differently. A frame loom has the warp as one continuous thread, while a weighted warp loom allows the individual warp threads to hang free. Both of these looms are inexpensive, easy to make, and take up very little space. They are also based on patterns that are thousands of years old.

## Make a Frame Loom

A simple frame loom can be made from any type of pipe. The one shown here is made from copper pipe, although you can also use PVC pipe. The directions are for an 18-inch weaving surface, although you can vary the size of the loom by using different lengths of pipe for the side, top, and bottom bars.

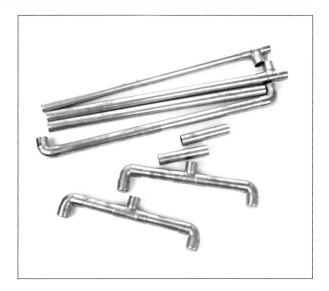

To start, you need the following supplies:

- an 8-foot length of ¾-inch residential-grade rigid copper pipe
- a pipe cutter
- a roll of plastic wrap
- four ¾-inch copper T's
- four ¾-inch copper street elbows
- two ¾-inch copper 90-degree elbows
- four ¾-inch caps

Cut six 4-inch pieces of copper pipe and four 18-inch pieces.

## TIP

Pipe cutters are inexpensive and surprisingly easy to use. However, if you don't want to cut the pipe yourself, some hardware stores can cut it to length for you.

## ASSEMBLE THE LOOM

1 Attach the two 90-degree elbows to either end of one of the 18-inch pipes.

2 Place an 18-inch pipe in each of the open ends of the 90-degree elbows.

3 Attach a T to each open end of the 18-inch pipes. Use the long end of the T's.

4 Place the remaining 18-inch length of pipe into the short ends of the T to form a square.

5 Place a 4-inch piece of pipe into the open ends of the attached T's.

6 Attach a T to both of these 4-inch pieces using the short end of the T.

7 Secure the remaining four pieces of 4-inch pipe into the ends of the T's.

8 Place the caps on the street elbows and place the street elbows on the open ends of the 4-inch pieces. These will form the feet on the loom.

9 Wrap a small square of plastic wrap over the ends of the pipes to hold the fittings firmly in place. The plastic wrap will hold the pipe together as if it had been glued, but you'll still be able to take it apart to adjust the size of the loom.

10 Make sure that everything is snug and even.

### Warp the Frame Loom

The next step is to warp the loom. The *warp* is the threads that are stretched lengthwise on the loom. The *weft* is the threads that are woven across the warp.

Depending on what you are weaving, you can use either your own handspun or a commercial yarn for the warp. The warp shown here is a commercial rug warp that is strong and fairly coarse. It is the perfect warp for weaving a pillow cover with handspun, because the handspun will completely cover the warp. To warp the frame loom, follow these steps:

1 Roll your warp yarn into a ball.

2 Tie one end on the top of the frame of the loom.

3 Wind the warp around the frame of the loom.

4 Keep the warp firm and even.

*CONTINUED ON NEXT PAGE*

## TWINE YOUR WARP

You will have threads on both the front and back of the loom. You can bring both of these sets of threads together with a weaving technique called *twining*.

To twine your warp, you need a length of strong cotton yarn that is three times the width of the loom. Follow these steps:

**1** Fold the cotton yarn in half.

**2** Loop the yarn around the frame just above the bottom bar. Pull it tight.

**3** Twine the cotton yarn through the warp by taking one warp thread from the front, slipping it between the pair of cotton yarns, twisting the cotton yarns together, and picking up the back thread.

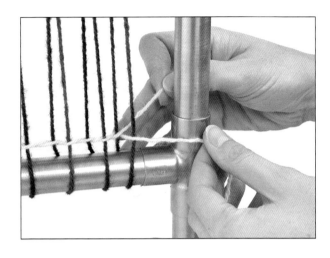

**4** Slip the back thread between the pair of cotton yarns.

**5** Give the cotton yarns a twist.

**6** Continue picking up one warp thread from the back and one from the front all the way across the warp.

This cotton thread is taken out when you finish weaving.

This warp is perfect for thick, handspun yarn. When you are weaving, you should pack the handspun tight with a tapestry beater or a kitchen fork. This ensures that the handspun covers the warp.

## Make a Weighted Warp Loom

A weighted warp loom is perfect for textured yarns. Unlike a traditional loom, where the warp is wound tightly onto the loom through a series of heddles and a reed that separate and lift different groups of threads, the warp hangs free and is moved by hand. Although this loom does limit the length of the fabric that you can weave, it allows you to put many more interesting yarns in the warp. It is simple and inexpensive to make (less than $10), and it takes up no more space than a window blind.

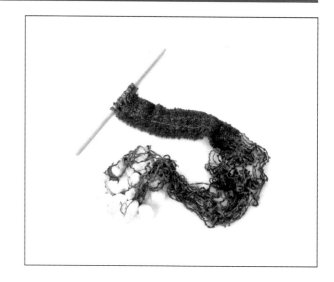

### GATHER UP THE PARTS

Here is what you need to make a weighted warp loom:

- a 2-inch wooden dowel cut to 5 feet long
- two bungee cords approximately 2 feet long, or any strong cord
- a roll of plastic wrap
- a ball of string
- a box of course salt or a bag of aquarium gravel
- a selection of handspun yarns—the more textured and varied, the better for the warp
- some finer yarns for the weft—commercial mohair yarns work well

*CONTINUED ON NEXT PAGE*

Portable clothes racks make a great weighted warp loom—just use the rack instead of a dowel. Attach the warp directly to the top of the rack.

## ASSEMBLE THE LOOM

1 Find a convenient place to hang your dowel with the bungees or the strong cord—for example, you can hang it from a curtain rod, an unused doorway, or between a pair of shelving units. If you can, mount two curtain-rod brackets on a wall and hang the rod from them. Make sure that the rod is hanging evenly.

2 Measure how long you want your project to be. Double this number and add 10 inches. Cut your handspun to this length.

3 Fold a length of the handspun in half.

4 Place the loop over the dowel, push the two loose ends through the loop, and pull the yarn snugly in place around the dowel.

5 Repeat steps 3 and 4 to place as many lengths of yarn across the dowel as you need for the width of the project. You can use a variety of sizes and textures. In this example, the scarf is 8 inches wide.

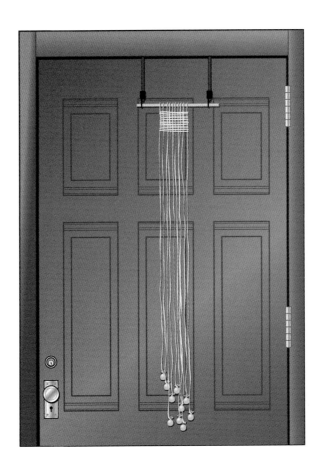

## MAKE THE WEIGHTS

1. Cut a square of plastic wrap for each warp end.

2. Place approximately 1 to 1½ ounces of salt or gravel on the plastic wrap.

3. Fold the plastic wrap around the salt or gravel, and tie it up with the string.

4. Attach a bag to each warp. Make sure that the weights are hanging free. If the warp doesn't clear the floor, wrap it around the bag.

These weights are reusable, and you can be creative with them. For example, you can make decorative cloth bags or bundles of metal, clay, or beads. The weights just need to weigh roughly the same amount.

### Ready to Weave

1. Check the spacing on the warp. If the threads look too close together for the fabric that you want to weave, slide them apart. If they look too loose, push them together.

2. Lift the warp threads with your fingers in the weaving pattern that you want to use. This scarf is being woven using a plain weave—one thread up, one thread down—because this simple structure shows off the texture of the handspun.

3. Enter the weft at the top of the warp. You can wind it into a small ball or around a flat weaving shuttle to keep it tidy.

4. Beat the weft in place with a tapestry beater or a kitchen fork. Unlike most modern looms, this weft is beaten up into the warp instead of down. For this scarf, a gentle beat works well. For rugs, a firmer beat works better (this is the same loom on which Vikings wove their rugs).

# appendix  A

# The Spinning Community

The spinning world is a wonderfully supportive community, and you will enjoy getting to know more about spinning and meeting people who share your love of fiber. This appendix gives you numerous spinning resources, including books, magazines, websites, and local resource options, as well as sheep- and wool-show event information.

**Suggested Reading** . . . . . . . . . . . . . . . . . . . . . . . . . . . . . . . . . . . . . . . .186

**Online Resources** . . . . . . . . . . . . . . . . . . . . . . . . . . . . . . . . . . . . .188

**Other Resources** . . . . . . . . . . . . . . . . . . . . . . . . . . . . . . . . . . . . . .189

# Suggested Reading

Here are a few reference books and magazines that you may want to use as you are learning to spin.

## Books

Amos, Alden. *The Alden Amos Big Book of Handspinning*. Interweave Press, 2001.

Boeger, Alexis. *Handspun Revolution*. Pluckyfluff Publishing, 2005.

Brown, Rachel. *The Weaving, Spinning, and Dyeing Book.* 2nd ed. Knopf Publishing, 1983.

Dean, Jenny. *Wild Color*. Watson-Guptill Publications, 1999.

Fannin, Allen. *Handspinning: Art and Technique*. Van Nostrand Reinhold, 1970.

Field, Anne. *The Ashford Book of Spinning*. Sterling Publishing Company, Inc., 1988.

Fournier, Nola and Jane Fournier. *In Sheep's Clothing: A Handspinner's Guide to Wool*. Reprint. Interweave Press, 2003.

Irwin, Bobbie. *The Spinner's Companion*. Interweave Press, 2001.

Kluger, Marilyn. *The Joy of Spinning*. Simon & Schuster, 1971.

Kroll, Carol. *The Whole Craft of Spinning: From the Raw Material to the Finished Yarn*. Dover Publications, 1981.

Menz, Deb. *Color in Spinning*. New edition. Interweave Press, 2005.

Raven, Lee. *Hands on Spinning*. Interweave Press, 1987.

Raven, Lee and Traci Bunkers. *Spin It: Making Yarn From Scratch.* Interweave Press, 2003, reprint from 1987.

Ross, Mabel. *The Encyclopedia of Handspinning*. US edition. Interweave Press, 1988.

Spin-Off Magazine, comp., *A Handspindle Treasury: 20 Years of Spinning Wisdom From Spin-Off Magazine.* Interweave Press, 2002.

Van Stralen, Trudy. *Indigo, Madder and Marigold: A portfolio of Colors from Natural Dyes.* Interweave Press, 1994.

Varney, Diane. *Spinning Designer Yarns.* Interweave Press, 2003.

## Magazines

### Fiberarts

*www.fiberarts.com*
201 E. Fourth St.
Loveland, CO 80537
(800) 875-6208

### Selvedge

*www.selvedge.org*
P.O. Box 40038
London
N6 5UW
+44 (0)208 341 9721

### Shuttle Spindle & Dyepot

*www.weavespindye.org*
1255 Buford Highway, Suite 211
Suwanee, Georgia 30024
(678) 730-0010

### Spindlicity

*www.spindlicity.com*
(online magazine)

### Spin-Off

*www.interweave.com/spin/spinoff_magazine/*
201 E. Fourth St.
Loveland, CO 80537
(800) 272-2193

### Wild Fibers

*www.wildfibersmagazine.com*
P.O. Box 1752
Rockland, ME 04841
(207) 785-3932

# Online Resources

You can find many spinning resources online, including fibers for sale, spinning how-to video clips, and equipment catalogs. There are even spinning blogs. Though none are listed below, many supplier sites often contain spinning "how-tos" and other resource information.

---

### www.weavespindye.org
**Handweavers Guild of America, Inc.**
The Handweavers Guild of America, Inc., aims to network weavers, spinners, dyers, basketmakers, fiber artists, and educators in order to increase awareness of and appreciation for the fiber arts. Their site provides information on local chapters, a calendar of events, and online issues of their award-winning quarterly publication, *Shuttle Spindle & Dyepot.*

### www.icanspin.com
**I Can Spin**
This site features free video clips that illustrate fiber preparation, spinning, and plying techniques.

### www.ansi.okstate.edu/breeds/sheep
**Oklahoma State University - Breeds of Livestock - Sheep Breeds**
Maintained by the Oklahoma State University department of animal science, this site lists many breeds of sheep giving the history of the breed, photos, and information about their fleece.

### www.spinweave.org
**Spinning and Weaving Association (SWA)**
SWA's site provides an extensive listing of retailers and wholesalers in the spinning and weaving industry, as well as other networking resources.

### http://community.livejournal.com/spinningfiber
**Spinningfiber (a LiveJournal Community)**
This open online community for spinning enthusiasts allows you to share tips and stories, to ask questions, and to just be around other people who understand the obsession.

### Textilelinks.com
This site lists links to teachers, events, and product and book reviews.

### www.yarnharlot.com
**Yarn Harlot Blog**
One of the most popular knitting blogs on the Web, the Yarn Harlot, aka Stephanie Pearl-McPhee, comments on life as a knitter and posts insightful how-tos on the fiber arts. Stephanie also spins—her wool eating squirrel stories and her advice on wool washing and storing are great.

In addition to books, magazines, and the Internet, you can often find spinning resources at your local yarn store. Here are some suggestions for finding local spinning resources, as well as a list of wool and sheep shows throughout the country.

## Local Resources

Your local yarn or weaving store is a good place to start. Even though they are not specifically stores for spinners, many of them carry spinning supplies and have a spinner on staff. Some stores have spinning circles that meet regularly.

Check the local Weaver's Guild; almost every guild has a spinner's group. The Handweaver's Guild of America (HGA), the umbrella organization for weavers' guilds in North America, offers a Certificate of Excellence in Spinning. Most guild conferences have workshops and seminars for spinners. HGA's website lists all of the guilds by area; for more information, visit www.fiberartsonline.com.

## Sheep and Wool Shows

Sheep and wool shows are great opportunities to meet suppliers and to try out equipment. Several major sheep and wool shows are held across the country every year. These shows feature classes, vendors, fleece and fiber sales, animals, craft demonstrations, and music. A sampling of shows is listed below, in calendar order.

For more on sheep and wool events, go online to www.woolfestival.com. This site showcases fiber events (festivals, workshops, and retreats) by date.

- **The Maryland Sheep and Wool Show**—outside of Baltimore. Early May.
- **Estes Park Wool Show**—Estes Park, Colorado. Third weekend in June.
- **The Black Sheep Gathering**—Eugene, Oregon. Third weekend in June.
- **Monterey Wool Show**—Monterey County, California. August.
- **Oregon Flock and Fiber**—Canby, Oregon. September.
- **New York State Sheep and Wool Festival**—Rhinebeck, New York. October.
- **S.O.A.R (Spin-Off Autumn Retreat)**—This is the one national spinning event, held yearly, for spinners. It rotates its location across the country and the dates vary between late September to early November. S.O.A.R. is run by Interweave Press, publisher of *Spin-Off* magazine.
- **Taos Wool Festival**—Taos, New Mexico. October.

# Spinning Reference Materials

As you spin, you will pick up on certain methods or techniques that work well for you. To help yourself, and your spinning friends, it is a good idea to write these techniques down. In this appendix, you will find a sample spinner's journal to illustrate how you can organize your notes. You will also find a list of common supplies that every spinner should have on hand.

**Keep a Spinner's Journal** . . . . . . . . . . . . . . . . . . . . . . . . . . . . . . .192

**In the Spinner's Closet** . . . . . . . . . . . . . . . . . . . . . . . . . . . . . . .194

One of the true benefits of spinning is that the process stimulates creative ideas. You can keep a journal or a sketchbook of your ideas, images, textures, and color inspirations.

You should keep a few simple art supplies on hand. A set of colored pencils and one or two colored ink pens are usually enough. A small hole punch, a small utility blade, and some transparent tape can help you to organize your samples.

Do not be intimidated by the blank page. This isn't meant to be art—it is a record of your ideas. By keeping good technical notes, you will develop a wonderful resource with which to plan future projects. These notes are also fun to share with your fiber friends.

You can use the fiber record on the next page as a guide (you may need to enlarge it on a photocopier), and add other information that you want to record. It is a good idea to store your fiber record pages in clear plastic cover sheets inside a ring binder.

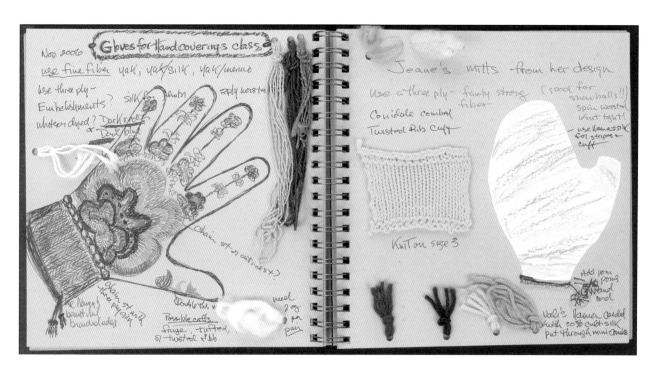

Fiber Record

**Fleece Sample:**
source:

condition:

skirted weight loss:

**Washing**
method:

weight loss:

**Processing**
method:

weight loss:

problems:

**Spinning**
method:

ply:

yardage:

**Structure**
method:

finishing:

changes?:

# In the Spinner's Closet

**Below is a checklist of items that every spinner should have on hand.**

---

- ❏ A lot of extra bobbins—you can't have too many. Because bobbins can be very expensive, an alternative is a weaver's bobbin winder and weaver's bobbins on which you can to store your finished singles.
- ❏ A color wheel. Most university bookstores and art supply stores stock these.
- ❏ A crockpot or two. These are great garage-sale finds. Crockpots are an easy way to scour fiber, especially mohair, and they also make good dye pots.
- ❏ A package of cloth-covered hair elastics. Keep these in your spinning basket, because they come in handy when you need to replace the spring on your spinning wheel. You can also use cloth-covered elastics to convert a box and a couple of knitting needles into a kate.
- ❏ Fine commercial yarn—ask for size 60/2 if you are buying it from a weaving supplier. Build up a range of fibers, including silk, cotton, fine wool, and rayon. Ignore the color; it can all be dyed.
- ❏ Hand cream. Rough spots on your hands are very annoying, especially when you are spinning fine fibers such as silk. A good trick is to rub your hands with a bit of fresh lemon. It makes your hands perfectly smooth for hours. You can also keep sesame seed oil in your spinning basket. It will make your hands smooth as well. An instant cure for rough hands is Cowboy Magic mane and tail detangler. Available at any ranch or horse supply store, a tiny bit of this conditioner will make your hands smooth in seconds.
- ❏ A McMorran balance. This clever tool measures how many yards there are in a pound of yarn, regardless of the size or the material. You can use it to record how many yards you have on hand for different spinning lots, or to match up yarn equivalents when you are using your handspun yarn with commercial knitting patterns. This tool is inexpensive and easy to use, and it comes with clear instructions.
- ❏ A salad spinner. This is another great garage-sale find. A salad spinner can extract excess water from fiber, skeins, and small finished projects.
- ❏ The proper tools to tighten all of the nuts, bolts, and screws on your spinning wheel. Keep these tools in your spinning basket. You can find compact, well-made tools at bicycle stores.
- ❏ Spinning wheel oil. Again, check the bicycle store. Mountain bike lubricants work well on spinning wheels.
- ❏ Extra drive-band material. Keep this material in your spinning basket.
- ❏ A small spray bottle for water to keep the static out of your spinning fiber.
- ❏ And, of course, fiber—you can't have too much! It will be your main source of inspiration.

# Glossary of Handspinning Terms

**analogous**  Colors that are side by side on the color wheel.

**attenuated long draw**  A variation of woolen spinning, in which the fiber is drafted back and extra twist is added. Also called *double drafting*.

**ball winder**  A tool used to wind yarn into a center-pull ball.

**bast fibers**  The skeletal structure of plants that is found in stems and leaves.

**batt**  Fiber that has been put through a drum carder and taken off in one big piece.

**bell**  A silk fiber preparation. A bell is many layers of either caps or hankies made from the silkworm cocoons that have been softened by boiling and then spread on a frame. A bell may be made from as many as 100 caps or hankies.

**binder**  Thread, usually fine, that is plied or cabled with a complex yarn or a tightly spun single to balance the twist. A binder is often used in bouclés to hold the loop structure in place.

**blocking**  A finishing technique that adds weight to a wet yarn while it is drying. It is used to take some of the twist out of a yarn and to reduce the yarn's elasticity.

**bobbin**  The part of the spinning wheel that holds the yarn during the spinning process.

**bobbin-driven wheel**  A type of single-drive spinning wheel where the drive band powers the bobbin; although it is the fastest of the three types, you have the least control when using this type of wheel.

**Bombyx mori**  A breed of silkworms bred in captivity that produces cultivated silk.

**bouclé**  Either yarn or fiber that has entered the plying process at right angles, thus forming a loop or a buckle in the yarn or fiber.

**cabling**  A spinning process in which two or more plied yarns are twisted together in the opposite direction to how they were plied.

**cap**    A silk fiber preparation. The silk cocoon is boiled (to soften it) and opened up, and the worm parts are cleaned out. Layer after layer of cocoons are stretched and dried on a frame. Silk caps are interesting to spin and are normally used by tailors for interfacing.

**chained ply**    See Navajo ply.

**complementary colors**    Hues that are directly opposite each other on a color wheel. For example, orange and blue are complementary colors. One color absorbs the reflective colors of the other.

**crimp**    The amount and type of waviness in a fiber. Natural fibers, such as wool, have a wide range of crimp. Synthetic fibers can be made to have different amounts of crimp.

**cultivated silk**    Silk that is grown from the silkworm *Bombyx mori.* These worms produce silk fiber that is fine and has a blue-white appearance.

**cut end**    The end of a fiber lock that was cut during shearing.

**dehair**    To remove the long, coarse outer hair or wool from animals such as bison, llama, and muskox, all of which have multiple coats.

**distaff**    A tool used to hold fiber while you spin.

**diz**    A tool used to pull off the fiber after it has gone through the top-making process. The size of the hole in the diz determines the size of yarn that can be spun from the top. Traditionally, a diz is made from horn, although it can be made from anything, including wood, plastic bottles, or shells.

**doffer**    A drum carder accessory used to open up the batt and free one end so it can be removed from the carder.

**double-drive wheel**    A type of spinning wheel in which both the bobbin and the flyer are run by the drive band. You have more control than when you use a bobbin-driven wheel, but less speed.

**draft**    A method used to pull a small amount of fibers out of the fiber bundle by hand during the spinning process.

**draw**    A method used to pull out the fiber that is to be spun.

**drive band**    A cotton cord or plastic band that connects the spinning wheel to the flyer and/or bobbin and makes them turn.

**drum carder**   A machine that opens and separates wool into spinning batts. Drum carders can be turned by hand or by an electric motor.

**encasement**   A spinning technique in which an unspun element—such as fiber, feathers, beads, or fabric—is caught between two or more yarns that are being plied together.

**English combs**   A set of two paddles, usually wooden, that have a number of metal tines set in rows. Each row is called a pitch and English combs generally have four pitches. English combs are used to prepare fibers for spinning by separating the broken, short, damaged fibers from the long, strong fibers. Using English combs produces top for spinning.

**felting**   A process that uses heat, lubrication, and agitation to force fibers closer together than they would normally be. Cold is then applied to shock the fibers so that they tighten down, thus locking the fibers close together. While this process is usually applied to sheep's wool, other animal fibers, such as camel, Angora rabbit, and alpaca, can also be felted.

**fiber hand**   The hand in which you hold the fiber while spinning.

**fiber reactive dye**   A dye that uses soda ash and salt to cause an interaction between the fiber and the dye. This dye is used on cellulose fibers and some synthetics, and can be modified to dye protein fibers.

**filaments**   Individual fibers of cultivated silk or other extruded fibers such as rayon and bamboo.

**flicker**   A tool that looks like (and often is) a dog brush, and that is used to brush open individual locks of fiber to prepare them for spinning.

**flyer**   The U-shaped part of a spinning wheel that winds the spun yarn around the bobbin.

**flyer-driven wheel**   A type of single-drive spinning wheel where the drive band powers the flyer and the bobbin is controlled with a scotch brake. This type of wheel gives you the most control over both the diameter of yarn that you spin and the amount of twist.

**footman**   The part of the spinning wheel that connects the treadle to the wheel.

**full**   A finishing technique that is used on either fabric or yarn made from fibers that are woolen spun. Hot water, soap, and agitation are used to mesh the fibers together. They are then shocked with a cold rinse and snapped or pounded to open all the fibers up. This process softens both fabric and yarn, and removes the extra twist that occurs in woolen spinning. Unlike felting, which this process closely resembles, the yarn usually becomes bigger rather than smaller when it is fulled.

**garnetted**   A method of carding that takes a woven or knit fabric or a yarn and pulls it apart so that it can be added back to fiber and re-spun. Garnetted yarns are made from recycled fabric and threads. A good example of a garnetted yarn is Donegal tweed.

**gauge**   The number of stitches per inch and the number of rows per inch in knitted fabric.

**hackle**   A comb without a handle.

**halo**   Textile term used to describe a fuzzy yarn, in which the fiber surrounds the core of the yarn, like a halo of light around a lamp. Angora and mohair yarns are examples of haloed yarns.

**hand cards**   Two paddles that have carding cloth attached to one side. They are used in pairs to open up short- to medium-length fiber before it is spun.

**hankies**   Silk fiber that has been processed from the cocoon. The process is the same as a silk cap (see also cap), but the form that the cocoon is stretched on is square, not the horseshoe shape used to produce caps.

**ikat**   A dye effect that leaves a repeatable mark where the dye could not penetrate the yarn. To achieve this effect, you intentionally tie the skeins too tightly.

**indigo**   A fermentation bath that is made from a number of different plants that contain a chemical called indicafloria.

**kate**   A tool used to hold spinning bobbins during the plying and cabling process. This is also known as a lazy kate.

**lace attachments**   Special bobbins and whorls that make it easier to spin both fine fibers and fine yarns.

**leader**   String or yarn that is attached to the spinning-wheel bobbin and that joins onto the fiber. The twist from the wheel is transferred to the leader and then to the fiber in the spinning process.

**licker in**   The front roller of a drum carder.

**linen**   Spun flax.

**locks**   Naturally occurring divisions in wool fiber.

**long draw**   A method of spinning in which the twist runs into unorganized fiber. This method is commonly used for short, carded fibers, and is also known as woolen spinning.

**maidens**   Two posts that hold the flyer in place on a spinning wheel.

**marl**   A spinning technique that mixes areas of solid and mixed colors in the yarn.

**McMorran balance**   A tool used to measure how many yards there are in a pound of yarn.

**mini-combs**   A set of two small hand-held paddles with one or two rows of tines. They are used to pre-pare fiber into top and for color blending.

**monochromatic**   A color system that uses one hue and then adds black, gray, and white to vary the hue.

**mordant**   A chemical salt used during the nature-dyeing process to bind the color to the fiber. Alum is a commonly used mordant.

**mother-of-all**   The part of the spinning wheel that holds the maidens, the flyer, the bobbin, and the whorls.

**nature dye**   Dye that is made from plants, minerals, or insects.

**Navajo ply**   Not actually a plied yarn, but a chained single that is twisted together. Once it has been twisted, it can be plied or cabled, but usually it is used just as a twisted chain. When colors are spun from multicolored singles, this plying technique is often used to prevent the colors from mixing too much. This technique is also called chained ply.

**niddy noddy**   A tool that is used to wind yarn into a skein. Most niddy noddies make 2-yard loop.

**nøstepinde**   A tool that is used to make a center-pull ball of yarn.

**orifice**   The opening on the flyer that the yarn passes through before it winds on the flyer.

**orifice hooks**   Wheel accessories used to thread the leader from the bobbin through the orifice on the flyer of the spinning wheel.

**overspun**   Spun yarn that contains too much twist to make a balanced yarn.

**over the fold**   A spinning method that is used with long, straight fibers to give them more loft and texture.

**pectin**   A natural glue that holds cellulose fibers together. Pectin can be dissolved in boiling water and harsh soap.

**pill**   Small bumps of broken fiber that felt on the surface of knitted fabric. Also called *neps.*

**ply**   Two or more singles that are spun together in the direction opposite to the original spinning twist. It is also the name of this method of spinning plying.

**plying heads**   Wheel accessories that increase both the diameter of the yarn you can spin and the amount of yarn you can have in a skein.

**puni**   Carded fiber that is rolled tightly around a stick.

**raw silk**   See silk noil.

**reeled silk**   Silk that is used to weave fabric just as it comes off of the cocoon.

**rolag**   Carded fiber after it comes off the hand cards. The fiber is rolled off the cards to make a soft and airy roll.

**roving**   Fiber that has been through the carding process. Roving contains fibers of uneven lengths and diameters, and the fibers are not in any set order.

**scotch brake**   A part on some single-drive-band spinning wheels that is used to apply pressure to the bobbin.

**scouring**   A dyeing-preparation method that eliminates all of the waxes and oils from fibers or yarns. Also used to describe the method of washing fiber before spinning.

**scurf**   A type of dandruff that is found in animal undercoats, such as from bison, Angora rabbits, yaks, and goats.

**semi-woolen**   A method of spinning that allows the twist to enter the fiber, but then stretches the fiber by drafting it toward the wheel.

**shade**   A color of yarn to which black has been added.

**shaft**   The part of the flyer that holds the bobbin.

**short draw**   A method of spinning that pulls the fibers out without letting the twist enter until it is under tension. This method is used for long fibers, such as silk, and for all fibers in top preparation.

**silk noil**   Short, broken silk fibers that are left on the carder when the cocoons are processed to make spinning fiber. This is also called raw silk.

**single**   Yarn with only one direction of twist.

**single-drive wheel**   This type of spinning wheel has only one drive band. Depending on the wheel, the drive band will turn the flyer ( flyer-driven wheel) or the bobbin (bobbin-driven wheel).

**skeining**   A technique in which you wind spun yarn in a series of layered circles. Yarn that has been skeined can be easily washed or dyed. When stored in a skein, the yarn won't lose its elasticity.

**slicker**   A tool that allows you to easily remove batts from drum carders, by lifting the fiber out of the carding teeth.

**slubs**   Large, uneven textures in yarn.

**spindle**   A simple tool used for spinning yarn. Made with a stick and a whorl that adds weight to keep the stick spinning, it has been used worldwide to make yarn.

**spinning hand**   The hand with which you control the twist while spinning.

**spiral yarn**   Yarn in which one single was held more loosely than the other during the plying process. The looser yarn makes a half loop around the tightly held yarn.

**strand**   A single portion of fiber. This term is also used to describe how many singles there are in a cabled yarn.

**Superwash**   Wool that has been treated chemically to prevent shrinking.

**supported draw**   Woolen spinning on a hand spindle.

**supported spindle**   A method of spinning in which the hand spindle is placed on a surface instead of hanging free. This method is used for spinning short fibers such as cotton or cashmere.

**swift**   A tool that holds a skein under tension so that you can wind it into a ball.

**teasing**   A fiber-preparation technique in which you gently pull the fiber apart with your fingers.

**tip end**   The end of the lock of fiber that is toward the outside of the fleece. Usually, the locks are spun from the tip end.

**tint**   A color of yarn to which white has been added.

**tone**   A color of yarn to which gray has been added.

**top**  Fiber that has been prepared for spinning by using combs to separate the long fibers from the short ones.

**treadle**  The pedal part of the spinning wheel. The treadle is pressed with the foot to make the wheel turn.

**tussah**  Any number of silks that are produced by wild silkworms. Although it naturally has a honey tone to it, it can also be bleached white.

**twice retted**  A short flax fiber with the silky look and feel of line fax.

**twining**  A weaving technique in which the weft is moved by hand to wrap completely around the warp.

**undercoat**  Short, soft animal fibers that shed out when the temperature rises. Cashmere, yak, and bison all have an undercoat.

**underspun**  Spun yarn that does not have enough twist to make the yarn that you want.

**warp**  The threads that are stretched lengthwise on the loom.

**weak acid dye**  A dye that uses vinegar or citric acid to bond the dye and the fiber together. This dye is only used for protein fibers.

**weft**  The threads that are woven across the warp.

**whorl**  The weight on the spindle. Bigger whorls spin bigger, lower-twist yarns, while smaller whorls spin smaller yarns with a higher twist. This term also describes the pulley system on a spinning wheel.

**wool combs**  Tools that are used to prepare fiber for spinning. They straighten and separate the fibers. They can also be used to blend colors.

**WooLee Winder**  A type of flyer that automatically winds the bobbin for you while you spin.

**woolen**  A method of spinning where the twist runs into unorganized fibers, after which the fiber is drafted out. This method is commonly used on short, crimpy fibers. Sometimes referred to as long draw.

**worsted**  A method of spinning that drafts the fibers out and enters the twist into fibers that are held parallel and under tension. This method is used for long, combed fibers and top. Sometimes it is referred to as short draw.

# Index

## A

acid dye, 156, 159–160, 161, 164, 202
alpaca fiber, 32, 138–139, 156
analogous colors, 168, 195
Angora goat fiber, 34
Angora rabbit fiber, 33, 86, 139, 140–142
animal fiber, 32–36
Ashford spinning wheels, 15, 16, 21
attenuated long draw, 147, 195

## B

Bactrian camel fiber, 33
balanced yarn, 88, 104
ball winders, 25, 66, 195
bamboo fiber, 38
bast fibers, 143–145, 195
batts, 25, 39, 195
bells, silk, 31, 150–151, 195
bias, knitting, 173
binder, 131, 195
bison fiber, 33, 86, 93, 152–153, 156
The Black Sheep Gathering, 189
bleaching bast fibers, 145
blended fibers, 38, 50
blocking, 93, 173, 195
blooming in the stitch, 96
bobbin-driven wheel, 15, 195
bobbins. *See also* WooLee Winder
    described, 14, 195
    emptying, 78–79
    filling, 77, 81
    freeing, 169
    need for, 194
    setting up, 70–71
    tensioning, 72–73, 75, 76
boiled-wool techniques, 93
*Bombyx mori*, 31, 195
books, spinning, 186
bottom whorl spindles, 9
bouclé yarn
    characteristics, 91, 118, 128, 195
    fibers for, 91, 128, 131, 149
    finishing, 93
    plying, 91
    push-up, 132
    silk, 131
    spinning, 128–130, 131
boxes, 45
bulky yarns, wheel type for, 15

## C

cable sweaters, yarn for, 96
cabling
    advantages, 106, 109
    defined, 106, 195
    with hand spindle, 110–111
    with spinning wheel, 112–113
    troubleshooting, 115
    uses, 106, 109
    yarn for, 108–109, 114, 144
camel fiber, 33, 148
caps, silk, 31, 150–151, 196
carding. *See also* garnetted fiber/yarn
    cotton fiber, 146
    dyed fiber, 168
    fiber preparation, 48–50, 51–53, 86
    reasons, 39
    techniques, 50, 51–53, 146
    tools, 25, 50–51, 53, 146, 197–198
carding cloth, 50
cashmere fiber, 34, 86, 93, 148, 156
cellulose fibers
    dyeing, 156, 160–161, 164, 165
    types, 37
chained ply, 121–123, 167, 199
chairs, spinning, 20
clothes racks as warp looms, 181
cochineal, 163
colors, designing, 168
color wheels, 194
combing
    damp fibers, 43
    English, 45–47, 197
    mini-, 44, 199
    reasons, 40, 84
    techniques, 44–47
    tools, 24, 45, 47, 197
    wool, 24, 202
commercial yarns, 114, 194
complementary colors, 168, 196
cotton fiber, 37, 146–147, 156
cotton hand cards, 146
Cowboy Magic mane and tail detangler, 194
crankshaft, 14
crimp, 196
crockpots, 157, 164, 165, 194
cultivated silk, 31, 150, 151, 196
cut ends, 43, 196

## D

dehairing, 139, 152, 196
distaffs, 22, 196
diz, 22, 46–47, 152, 196
doffers, 52, 196
dog brushes, 24
dog hair fiber, 34, 148, 156
double-drive wheels
    described, 16, 196
    drive band placement, 71
    setting up, 69
    tensioning bobbin, 73, 76
    troubleshooting, 81, 115
down fibers, 148
drafting, 88, 89, 196

drawing, 196
drive bands
     changing, 18
     described, 14, 18, 196
     maintenance, 23, 194
     setting up, 69–70
     tensioning, 14, 73, 80, 81
drive band tensioner, 14
drop spindles, 8
drum carding, 25, 51–53, 197
dyed materials
     carding, 168
     plying, 169
     spinning, 166–167
dyeing
     alpaca, 156
     cellulose fibers, 156, 160–161, 164, 165
     dog hair, 156
     dye types, 156
     fiber reactive technique, 156, 160–161, 164, 197
     flax, 37, 156
     hemp, 156
     mohair, 34
     natural dyes, 156, 161, 162–163, 199
     novelty techniques, 164–165, 167
     preparing fiber for, 39, 158
     process, 159–162
     Procion dyes, 156
     protein fibers, 164, 165
     qiviut, 36
     ramie, 156
     roving, 167
     silk, 31, 156
     singles, 96
     soy, 156
     space/tools for, 157
     storing leftover dye, 161
     synthetic fibers, 156
     tea dye, 163
     weak acid method, 156, 159–160, 161, 164, 202
     wool/woolen yarns, 29, 156
     yak, 35
dye pots, 157

**E**

electric spinning wheels, 15
encased yarns, 135, 149
encasement, 197
ends, lost, 81
English Angora rabbit fiber, 33, 140
English combing, 45–47, 197
Estes Park Wool Show, 189
eucalyptus fiber, 38
events, sheep and wool, 189

**F**

felting, 29, 84, 93, 197
festivals, sheep and wool, 189

*Fiberarts*, 187
fiber hand, 56, 197
fiber preparation, 43–53. **See also** carding; combing
fiber reactive dye, 156, 160–161, 164, 197
fiber record, 192–193
fibers. **See also** *individual fibers*
     blended, 38, 50
     buying, 39–40
     classifications, 28
     stash, 39–41
     storing, 41
     types, 28
     using unusual, 5
     washing, 41–42
filaments, silk, 31, 197
finishing. **See also** fulling
     Angora rabbit fiber, 141–142
     bast fibers, 144–145
     blocking, 93, 173, 195
     cotton, 147
     down fibers, 148
     tools, 93
     woolen yarns, 88, 92
     worsted yarns, 92
five-ply yarn, 96
flame yarn, 125
flax fiber, 37, 84, 156. **See also** bast fibers
flickers, 24, 43, 197
flyer, 14, 69, 70, 77, 197
flyer-driven wheels, 16, 197
footman, 14, 80, 197
forks, 24
frame looms, 178–180
French Angora rabbit fiber, 33, 140
fulling
     advantages, 114
     Angora rabbit fiber, 141–142
     bison/qiviut fiber, 153
     down fiber, 148
     process, 92–93, 197

**G**

garnetted fiber/yarn, 38, 50, 133–134, 198
gauge, stitch, 172, 174, 198
German Angora rabbit fiber, 33, 140
goat fiber, 34–35, 149

**H**

hackles, 47, 198
hair elastics, 12, 96, 194
half-hitch knot, 61
halo, 139, 198
hand carding, 25, 48–50, 198
hand cream, 194
hands
     caring for, 194
     characteristics, 56
     dominance, 56, 58

fiber hand, 56, 197
  spinning hand, 56, 201
  warming up/stretching, 57–58
hand spindles
  attaching leaders, 59
  bison/qiviut fiber, 153
  cabling with, 110–111
  cotton fiber, 147
  described, 8–13, 201
  flame yarn, 125
  garnetted yarn, 133
  history, 56
  making, 12–13
  marled yarn, 119
  Navajo ply, 122
  parts, 10
  plying, 99–100
  selecting, 10–11
  setting up, 59–61
  spinning techniques, 8, 62–64
  troubleshooting, 65–66
  Turkish knot yarn, 125
  types, 8, 9, 201
  whorls on, 9, 10
  winding yarn onto/off of, 64–65, 66
  woolen yarns, 89
Handweaver's Guild of America (HGA), 188, 189
hankies, silk, 31, 150–151, 198
heat sources for dyeing, 157
hemp fiber, 37, 156. *See also* bast fibers
HGA (Handweaver's Guild of America), 188, 189
high-whorl spindles, 9
history of spinning, 4–5, 14, 15, 16, 56
holographic fiber, 38
hooks, 14, 19
Huacaya alpaca, 32

**I**

I Can Spin website, 188
ikat, 158, 198
indicafloria, 163
indigo, 163, 198
"in the grease" locks, 43, 44

**J**

Jensen spinning wheel, 16
journals, spinning, 192–193
jumbo heads, 21

**K**

kates, 20, 97, 198
knitting, 172–177, 198

**L**

lace
  spinning attachments, 21, 198
  yarn for, 84, 96
lanolin, 42

lark's-head knot, 71
leaders, 59, 71–72, 198
lead string, 10
lemon, use on hands, 194
Lendrum playing head, 21
Lendrum wheels, 19, 21
*Letheria vulpina*, 163
lichen, 163
licker in, 53, 198
lighting for dyeing, 157
line flax, 37
linen, 37, 198. ***See also*** flax fiber
llama fiber, 35, 138–139
locks, 128, 198
long draw spinning, 87–88, 198
looms, 178–180, 181–183
Louet S10 spinning wheel, 15
low-whorl spindles, 9

**M**

magazines, spinning, 187
Magicraft wheel, 19
maidens, 14, 70, 199
maintenance, wheel, 23, 194
marled yarn, 119–120, 199
Maryland Sheep and Wool Show, 189
Matchless Schacht wheel, 21
McMorran balance, 174–175, 194, 199
metalized fiber, 38
microfiber, 38
mid-whorl spindles, 9
milk fiber, 38
mini-combs, 44, 199
mohair fiber, 34, 42, 139, 149, 166
monochromatic colors, 168, 199
Monterey Wool Show, 189
mordant, 156, 162, 199
mother-of-all, 14, 17, 70, 199
moths, 41
multicolored balls dyeing technique, 165, 167
multiple plied yarn, 96, 103. ***See also*** plying
muskox fiber, 36, 152–153
Mylar fiber, 38

**N**

nature dye, 156, 161, 162–163, 199
Navajo ply, 121–123, 167, 199
Navajo spinning techniques, 89
neps, 173, 200
New York State Sheep and Wool Festival, 189
niddy noddies, 21, 25, 78, 199
nøstepinde, 25, 66, 98, 199
novelty yarns. ***See also*** *individual types*
  advantages, 116, 118
  characteristics, 116, 118
  dyeing techniques for fibers, 165
  wheel type for, 15
nylon fiber, 38

## O

oiling, wheel, 23, 194
Oklahoma State University Sheep Breeds website, 188
online resources, 188
Oregon Flock and Fiber, 189
orifice, 14, 19, 199
orifice hooks, 22, 72, 199
Ott-Lite, 157
overspinning, 65, 76, 199
over the fold method, 138, 199

## P

painted roving dyeing technique, 164–165, 167
pectin, 199
Pendleton Woolen Mills, 134
pill, 173, 200
pipe cutters, 178
pitches, 45
plying
    advantages, 94, 96
    Angora yarn, 140
    bast fibers, 144
    bouclé yarn, 91
    colored materials, 169
    described, 94, 200
    dyed materials, 169
    goat fiber, 149
    on hand spindles, 99–100, 122
    joining singles, 104
    multiple plies, 96, 103
    Navajo ply, 121–123, 167, 199
    from painted balls, 167
    silk, 150, 151
    slub yarns, 90
    on spinning wheels, 15, 101–102, 112, 122
    three-ply, 103
    tools, 20, 21, 97, 103, 104
    troubleshooting, 104–105
    two-ply, 99–102
plying balls, 98
plying heads, 21, 200
preparation, spinner, 57–58
Procion dye, 156
protein fibers, 29–36, 164, 165
punis, 49, 146, 200
pygora goat fiber, 35, 149

## Q

qiviut fiber, 36, 152–153

## R

rainbow pot dyeing technique, 164, 166
ramie fiber, 37, 156. *See also* bast fibers
raw fiber, 39
raw silk, 32, 200
recordkeeping, 192–193

recycled fiber, 38
reeled silk, 31, 200
re-plying, 110, 112
resources, spinning, 186–187, 188, 189
rolags, 49, 146, 200
roving, 39, 40, 86, 167, 200

## S

salad spinners, 41, 92, 93, 140, 194
sari waste fiber, 38
scotch brakes
    adjusting, 73, 76, 80, 81, 115
    described, 14, 16, 200
scouring, 39, 158, 200
scurf, 36, 200
seaweed fiber, 38
seed yarn, 124
*Selvedge*, 187
semi-woolen method, 140, 148, 200
sesame seed oil, use on hands, 194
Shacht spinning wheel, 16
shade, 168, 200
shaft, 10, 200
sheep
    breeds website, 188
    shows, 189
    wool from, 30
short draw method, 200
shows, sheep and wool, 189
*Shuttle Spindle & Dyepot*, 187
silk
    characteristics, 31, 32, 150
    drafting, 151
    dyeing, 156
    handling/storing unspun, 151
    materials for spinning, 150–151
    plying, 150, 151
    spinning, 151
    tussah, 32, 150, 151, 202
    types, 31–32
    for worsted yarn, 84
silk noil, 32, 201
single-drive wheels, 69, 73, 76, 201
singles, 65, 96, 123, 201
skeins, 78–79, 158, 201
sketchbooks, 192–193
slickers, 52, 201
slipknot, 59–60
slubs, 81, 201
slub yarns, 90, 93
S.O.A.R (Spin-Off Autumn Retreat), 189
social benefits, 5
soy fiber, 38, 156
specialty fibers, 38
spindles. *See* hand spindles
*Spindlicity*, 187

Spinning and Weaving Association (SWA), 188
Spinningfiber online community, 188
spinning hand, 56, 201
spinning wheels. *See also* double-drive wheels
 adjusting, 69
 bouclé yarn on, 128–130, 131
 bulky yarns on, 15
 cabling with, 112–113
 history, 14, 15, 16
 leaders, attaching, 71–72
 maintenance, 23, 194
 novelty yarns on, 15
 parts, 14
 for plying, 15, 101–102, 112, 122
 selecting, 17–19
 setting up, 69–73
 single-drive, 69, 73, 76, 201
 tension, adjusting, 72–73, 75, 76
 travel bags, 21
 troubleshooting, 76, 80–81
 types, 15–16, 18–19, 21, 195, 197
 woolen yarns on, 87–88
 wrapped spiral yarn, 124
*Spin-Off*, 187
Spin-Off Autumn Retreat (S.O.A.R.), 189
SpinTek spinning wheel, 15
spiral yarn, 201
split complement colors, 168
squirrel cage swift, 22
stash, fiber, 39–41
static, preventing, 194
storage rack, 14
storing fibers, 41
strand, 201
stress relief, 5
suint, 42
Superwash, 29, 201
supplies, 192, 194
supported draw, 89, 201
supported spindles, 8, 201
Suri alpaca, 32
SWA (Spinning and Weaving Association), 188
swifts, 22, 201
synthetic fibers, 38, 156

**T**

Taos Wool Festival, 189
tea dye, 163
teasing, 43, 201
Textilelinks.com website, 188
textured yarn, 124–127
three-ply yarn, 96. *See also* plying
tint, 168, 202
tip end, 201
tips, 43

tone, 168, 202
tools. *See also* hand spindles; spinning wheels
 processing, 24–25, 194
 spinning, 20–22, 194
 wheel maintenance, 194
top, 40, 84, 123, 202
top whorl spindles, 9
tow flax, 37
travel bags, 21
treadles, 14, 18, 202
treadling, 67–68, 76, 80
troubleshooting
 cabling, 115
 hand spindles, 65–66
 knitting, 173
 plying, 104–105
 spinning wheels, 76, 80–81, 115
Turkish knot yarn, 125–127
tussah silk, 32, 150, 151, 202
twice retted flax, 37, 202
twining, 180, 202
twist
 adjusting, 64, 65, 66
 checking, 65
 identifying, 127
two-ply yarn, 96. *See also* plying

**U**

umbrella swift, 22
undercoat, 36, 202
underspinning, 66, 76, 202

**W**

warp, 179, 180–183, 202
washing, 41–42
washing soda, 144
weak acid dye, 156, 159–160, 161, 164, 202
wearability, checking yarn, 173
Weaver's Guilds, 189
weaving
 frame looms, 179–180
 weighted warp looms, 181–183
 yarn for, 84, 86, 96, 138
 yarn preparation, 93
weft, 179, 202
weighted warp looms, 181–183
wheel, 14
whorls
 choosing, 104
 described, 8, 14, 15, 202
 hand spindle, 9, 10
 making, 12
 troubleshooting, 81
 using, 69, 70, 71
*Wild Fibers*, 187

wool
- care, 29
- characteristics, 29
- combing, 24, 202
- dyeing, 29, 156
- events for, 189
- fibers for worsted yarns, 84
- preparing fiber, 24, 202
- types, 30
- washing, 42

wool combs, 24, 202
WooLee Winder, 20, 202
woolen yarns
- characteristics, 82, 86, 88
- dyeing, 29, 156
- fiber preparation, 86
- fibers for, 86
- finishing, 88, 92
- spinning, 87–88, 89, 202

wool shows, 189

worsted yarns
- characteristics, 82, 84
- fiber preparation, 84
- fibers for, 84, 86
- finishing, 92
- spinning, 85, 202

wrapped spiral yarn, 118, 124

## Y

yak fiber, 35, 86, 93
yarn. *See also* *specific types*
- blocking, 93, 173, 195
- creating unusual, 5
- measuring, 174–175, 194, 199
- wearability, 173

Yarn Harlot Blog, 188

# Teach Yourself VISUALLY™ books...

Whether you want to knit, sew, or crochet...strum a guitar or play the piano...train a dog or create a scrapbook...make the most of Windows XP or touch up your Photoshop CS2 skills, Teach Yourself VISUALLY books get you into action instead of bogging you down in lengthy instructions. All Teach Yourself VISUALLY books are written by experts on the subject and feature:

- Hundreds of color photos or screenshots that demonstrate each step or skill

- Step-by-step instructions accompanying each photo
- FAQs that answer common questions and suggest solutions to common problems
- Information about each skill clearly presented on a two- or four-page spread so you can learn by seeing and doing
- A design that makes it easy to review a particular topic

Look for Teach Yourself VISUALLY books to help you learn a variety of skills—all with the proven visual learning approaches you enjoyed in this book.

0-7645-9641-1

## Teach Yourself VISUALLY™ Crocheting

Picture yourself crocheting accessories, garments, and great home décor items. It's a relaxing hobby, and this is the relaxing way to learn! This Visual guide *shows* you the basics, beginning with the tools and materials needed and the basic stitches, then progresses through following patterns, creating motifs and fun shapes, and finishing details. A variety of patterns gets you started, and more advanced patterns get you hooked!

0-7645-9640-3

## Teach Yourself VISUALLY™ Knitting

Get yourself some yarn and needles and get clicking! This Visual guide *shows* you the basics of knitting—photo by photo and stitch by stitch. You begin with the basic knit and purl patterns and advance to bobbles, knots, cables, openwork, and finishing techniques—knitting as you go. With fun, innovative patterns from top designer Sharon Turner, you'll be creating masterpieces in no time!

0-7645-9642-X

## Teach Yourself VISUALLY™ Guitar

Pick up this book and a guitar and start strumming! *Teach Yourself VISUALLY Guitar* shows you the basics photo by photo and note by note. You begin with essential chords and techniques and progress through suspensions, bass runs, hammer-ons, and barre chords. As you learn to read chord charts, tablature, and lead sheets, you can play any number of songs, from rock to folk to country. The chord chart and scale appendices are ready references for use long after you master the basics.

# designed for visual learners like you!

0-7645-7927-4

## Teach Yourself VISUALLY™ Windows® XP, 2nd Edition

Clear step-by-step screenshots *show* you how to tackle more than 150 Windows XP tasks. Learn how to draw, fill, and edit shapes, set up and secure an Internet account, load images from a digital camera, copy tracks from music CDs, defragment your hard drive, and more.

0-7645-8840-0

## Teach Yourself VISUALLY™ Photoshop® CS2

Clear step-by-step screenshots *show* you how to tackle more than 150 Photoshop CS2 tasks. Learn how to import images from digital cameras, repair damaged photos, browse and sort images in Bridge, change image size and resolution, paint and draw with color, create duotone images, apply layer and filter effects, and more.

Visual®
An Imprint of ⊕WILEY
Now you know.